Brewing Saké

Release the Toji Within

William G Auld

Brewing Saké

Copyright © 2012 by William G Auld

All rights reserved. No part of this book may be reproduced or transmitted in any form or by any means without written permission of the author.

ISBN-13: 978-1468147780

ISBN-10: 1468147781

Cover by Gabriel W. Auld.

Photography by Maya A. Auld.

I dedicate this book to my wife Yuli, my son Gabe and my daughter Maya for their help, encouragement and love.

Acknowledgments

This book was inspired by several people, all of whom I admire. The first among these is Fred Eckhardt. Most high quality homebrew saké leads back to him in one form or another. He wrote the book "SAKE (U.S.A.)" which presented the first widely available high quality saké recipe and procedure outside of Japan. Both before and after publishing his book he taught people to brew fine saké and continued to update his recipe for all. I was lucky that we were both in Portland where I was able to talk with Fred and get his insights.

Next is John Gauntner, the number one English speaking teacher of all things Saké. First through John's writing and then through his class, I learned about saké and those involved in the industry. He gave me a much deeper understanding of the history and tradition that play a huge part of why saké is what it is.

Four others who substantially influenced my understanding of saké and helped point me in the right direction were Yasutaka Daimon, Sachiko Furukawa, Marcus Pakiser and Ad Blankestijn.

Then there is Jonathan Musther who patiently worked with me on chemistry and its application to saké.

To each of you I say thank you.

Preface

In this book I want to provide you with the knowledge and ability to brew your own high quality saké that you will enjoy and be proud to share. There is no other book like this in English or any other language other than Japanese. There are several books on saké and most discuss basic saké brewing procedures to some extent. However, this book is entirely dedicated to saké brewing for homebrewers.

Here we will learn about all the ingredients and the equipment needed for brewing saké. We will explore the brewing procedure in detail from start to finish. This will begin with a step by step method that will give you the best chance of a successful first brew. By the time you have finished reading this book you will have a full command and understanding of saké brewing.

Additional information about saké can be found at my web site: **HomeBrewSake.com**

Table of Contents

Introduction 1

How Saké is Brewed 5

Brewing Equipment 11

Quick Start Saké Brewing 25

Rice – Kome (米) 39

Koji (麹) 49

Yeast – Kobo (酵母) 59

Water – Mizu (水) 67

Nihonshu-do (日本酒度) or Saké Meter Value (SMV) ... 73

Sando (酸度) – Acidity 79

Amino Sando (アミノ酸度) – Amino Acid 81

Protecting your Homebrew Saké from light 83

Sanitation 85

Seimai (精米) or Rice Milling / Polishing 89

Rice Preparation 101

Koji Making 105

The Moto 111

The Buildup - San-Dan-Jikomi (三段仕込み) 135

The Main Ferment - Moromi (諸味) 145

So you like the Honjozo (本醸造) 151

Time for Shibori (搾り) 157
Final Steps in Saké Brewing 161
Measuring Your Homebrew Saké 165
Spoilers and Trouble Shooting 191
Glossary 193
Links and Contacts 211

Introduction

This book will focus on brewing Seishu; the official name for Saké in Japan. I make this distinction because, while outside of Japan, Saké is synonymous with seishu, it is not within Japan. Within Japan, saké is the term used for any kind of alcohol, while seishu or Nihon-shu is the Japanese saké.

Saké is made with four ingredients: rice, koji, yeast and water. All, except the koji, are familiar to most people. Koji is a mold culture grown on rice in the case of Saké. The mold is Aspergillus oryzae. It forms a white fluffy coating over the rice and excretes enzymes which convert the rice starch into sugar. This is the primary function of koji in brewing saké; to provide enough enzymes to convert the starch provided by the rice to sugar. Other compounds produced by the koji contribute to the final taste.

Once the koji enzymes convert the starch from the rice to sugar, yeast converts the sugar to alcohol. Beyond this major contribution the yeast also produce other compounds that contribute to the final taste and aroma of the saké. These two processes, conversion of starch to sugar and conversion of sugar to alcohol, proceed at the same time which allows the yeast to produce higher levels of alcohol than is the usual case in beer and wine. This is not to say that beer and wine cannot ferment to the high levels that saké does but that special processes, outside the norm, are needed to obtain the same high level normally reached with saké.

Short, fat grains of rice are preferable for making saké. These grains have a nice big ball of starch in the middle. The outer layers of a grain of rice contain a higher concentration of lipids, proteins, and fat than the inner parts of the grain. The lipids, proteins and fat produce undesirable flavors in saké so the outer layers are removed in a milling process. Table rice (white rice) is produced by milling brown rice down to around 90% to 93% of its original size. Because the milling rate holds so much sway over saké, it has been chosen as a key factor in the classification of saké grades. In addition to milling level, additives are also an important factor in the classification. The most common categories of saké are:

- Sanzo Shu is the majority of saké produced. San means three and implies that 3x the added alcohol is used along with various other additions.
- Futsu Shu is most commonly made of rice milled to between 93% and 70%. It usually includes additional alcohol and often has other additives.
- Honjozo is saké with added alcohol (not to exceed 10% of rice by weight) and a milling leaving no more than 70% of original.
- Junmai means pure rice. Specifically, pure rice signifies that no brewer's alcohol or anything else is added. Prior to Jan. 1, 2004, the rice also had to be milled leaving no more than 70% of original, but since 2004 the milling rate is no longer specific. However the rate of milling must be printed on the bottle.
- Ginjo is the same as Honjozo accept the rice must be milled leaving no more than 60% of the original.
- Junmai Ginjo is the same as Junmai accept the rice must be milled such that no more than 60% of the original rice remains.
- Daiginjo is Ginjo with rice milled so that no more than 50% of original remains.
- Junmai Daiginjo is Junmai Ginjo milled such that no more than 50% of the original rice remains.

The first two of these, Sanzo shu and Futsu shu are normal or table saké while the last 6 make up the categories of special designation saké. Special designation saké is not allowed to have anything added other than rice, koji, water, yeast and alcohol for those that are not Junmai.

Introduction

Water is extremely important to producing outstanding saké. It is very important that it contains as little iron and manganese as possible. The softer the water the less crisp, while harder water produces crisper saké. Adjustments may be made to transform the water to be more suitable to the type of saké desired.

While not mentioned as one of the four ingredients for making saké, lactic acid is most commonly added as well. When lactic acid is added to the moto, that is, the yeast starter, it is called sokujo moto. In more traditional moto styles, kimoto and yamahai moto, lactic acid is naturally produced by encouraging the growth of lactic acid producing bacteria, lactobacillus. This shift in process from kimoto or yamahai moto to sokujo moto shortens the time needed and provides more control on the amount of acid in the saké. In addition, because the lactic acid protects the moto from bacteria and fungi, when adding at the beginning of the moto, the resulting saké is generally cleaner tasting and has less risk of going bad.

So, how do these ingredients combine to make saké? Well, without going into too much detail let's make a quick run through the process. The first thing that needs to be done is to produce or get the koji. For now let's just start by assuming we have koji. This is true for many saké homebrewers so it is a good place to start. The next step in the process is to create the Moto or starter mash. This is the initial combining of ingredients. We start small because of the small amount of yeast we have to start and the yeast's inability to function properly in high concentrations of sugar. Starting with a small amount of koji and rice ensures that we don't get too much sugar before the yeast has enough time to multiply enough to handle the amount of sugar. After the Moto, there are three additions of rice, water, and koji, each roughly doubling in size. As with the Moto this gives the yeast time to multiply its population enough to handle the larger supply of sugar produced by the koji and rice. Once the additions have been added the Moromi begins. The Moromi is the main fermentation. Finally, the Yodan step generally used only for futsu and sanzo shu; this step involves a stabilizing addition of water, koji, and rice. And voila, we have saké; press, age condition, pasteurize and bottle.

How Saké is Brewed

Saké is brewed in a drawn out process that can take quite a long time but none of the individual steps are particularly difficult. In the traditional method, brewing saké starts with the rice and its milling. The objective is to remove the outer layers of the rice which cause saké to be less stable and to have harsher flavors. These layers contain the bran and the highest concentrations of oils, fatty acids, proteins and minerals like magnesium and iron. Table rice (white rice) is generally milled to between 90% and 93% of its original size. Sakemai (Saké Rice) is usually milled somewhere between 90% for futsu-shu (table saké) and 35% for the most refined Daiginjo. Removing the outer layer leads to a more stable and refined saké.

Once the rice has been milled to the proper level, we need to steam the rice. We use steamed rice both for making koji and to directly add to the brew. In order to steam the rice properly we need to first wash the milled rice to remove the outer layer of rice flower, talc or whatever may be on the rice. After a good washing the rice is soaked to absorb the needed amount of water for proper steaming. This amounts to about 30% by weight. The higher the milling rate the faster the rice will absorb the desired amount of water. Kurabito (brewery people) working with the most highly polished (milled) rice often use a stopwatch to time the soaking period so the rice does not take on too much moisture. Here the goal is to get enough moisture into the rice so that the steaming process gelatinizes the rice by heating the water already there. If the rice has too much moisture it will become soggy or mushy during the steaming process and will not form a nice home for koji. Also, soggy or mushy rice breaks down too easily, making a slow controlled fermentation less likely.

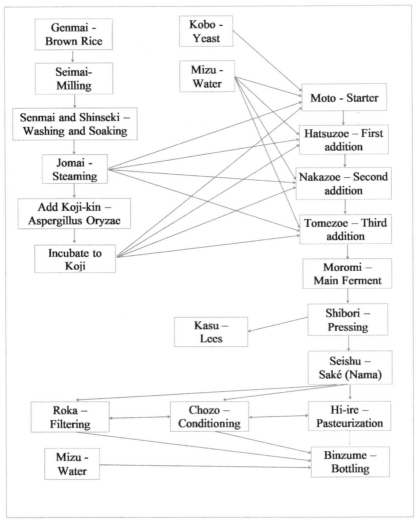

Figure 1: Saké Making Process

With the rice properly washed and soaked it can now be placed in the kettle for steaming. The kettle is lined with cloth and the rice is added in layers so the steam has natural diffusion layers. We don't want the steam to drill a tunnel through the rice thereby reaching only a small portion of the rice. Most brewers steam the rice for somewhere between 40 to 60 minutes. Once the steaming is complete, the rice should be firm and chewy without being overly sticky. At this stage the rice is either used for koji production or goes straight into the brew after cooling.

Steamed rice to be used for koji production is cooled down only to about 113°F (45°C) while it is being mixed and stirred to break up all chunks. When the rice is mostly chunk free and has cooled to 113°F, koji-kin (Aspergillus Oryzae) is sprinkled over the rice and mixed in to inoculate the rice. The mold is then cultivated over the next 44 to 54 hours to produce koji; the mold covered rice that looks like small fussy white pillows. Koji provides the enzymes that convert rice starch to sugar and break down proteins into peptides and amino acids. Having produced koji, it is time to create the moto, i.e., the yeast starter.

The moto is the initial starter for the brew. The most common method used for the moto is sokujo moto. Sokujo generally takes one to two weeks; beginning with koji, rice, yeast, lactic acid and water. All combined, the koji enzymes break down the starches to sugars and the yeast goes through a multistage process, first aerobic then anaerobic. In the aerobic stage the yeast build up their cell walls and then reproduce to create more yeast through a budding process. The cell wall build up and reproduction is important to have enough yeast in later stages where there is much more sugar to process. Next, the anaerobic stage, the yeast has used most of the oxygen in the moto and begins to process the sugar into alcohol and carbon dioxide. The anaerobic stage continues until virtually all the sugars have been consumed and there is no more being created by the enzymes working on the starch or the alcohol level is too high for the yeast.

The goals of the moto are multiple. First, the moto is to build up the needed yeast for the brew. Second, the moto is to provide lactic acid needed to protect the brew. In sokujo moto, lactic acid is added rather than cultivated. However, when using more traditional motos, the moto is used to cultivate the bacteria that provide the lactic acid and more complex character for the saké.

Once the moto is complete, a series of three additions are made to convert the moto into the moromi. These three additions are done over a period of 4 days. The three additions are:

- Hatsuzoe – the first addition, day 1
- Nakazoe – the second, middle, addition, day 3
- Tomezoe – the third and final addition, day 4

In each of these three additions, koji, steamed rice and water are added. Koji and water are added at the beginning of the period followed about 12 hours later by steamed rice and water. After Hatsuzoe a day of rest is allowed. This day of rest (day 2) is Odori (the dancing ferment). Odori is followed by Nakazoe and Tomezoe, each taking one day with additions of increasing size but with the same pattern as Hatsuzoe; koji and water followed by steamed rice and water 12 hours later.

With the end of Tomezoe, the main ferment, Moromi, begins. Having added all the koji, rice and water, it is now left to the enzymes and yeast to do the work. The yeast, as we mentioned above, go through stages, aerobic cell wall build up followed by reproduction through budding and anaerobic processing sugar into alcohol and carbon dioxide. They are mostly in the anaerobic stage at the end of moto but the introduction of the three additions along with continual stirring provides a complex environment where some yeast may be building cell walls, some budding and some producing alcohol. By the latter half of moromi, however, the yeast have almost completely settled into their anaerobic efforts, making alcohol.

Yeast are more efficient in their transformation process than are the enzymes in the moromi. As quickly as the enzymes create simple sugars yeast pick them up and convert them to alcohol and carbon dioxide. This produces a brew with very low levels of sugar which help the yeast to continue to remain healthy. High levels of sugar in solution are toxic for yeast. Moromi lasts for around 14 days to 30 days.

At the end of Moromi, the brew is pressed to force the saké from the kasu (lees). This removes much of the solids but not all. After settling, saké is filtered and pasteurized. At this point the saké is allowed to age and condition for a few months or more. When it is time for bottling an adjustment is often made to bring the alcohol level in line with standard sake; about 15% to 16%. Genshu is saké that has not had this adjustment made, leaving it at from 18% to 22%.

Once the Saké has aged for some time it is ready to be bottled. During bottling the saké is also pasteurized for a second time. This is to ensure that the enzymes are denatured and that the vast majority of bacteria and fungi have been destroyed. This stabilizes the sake. With the saké now bottled and pasteurized it is now ready to drink.

Brewing Equipment

What Equipment do we need to brew saké at home? Well, the equipment needed is, in most cases, readily available from home-brew shops. These shops are in most communities as well as online. Some examples will be given in the Links and Contacts section near the end of this book.

To keep this section as straightforward and clear as possible I will only give one example for most of the equipment. This does not mean the example shown is the best, cheapest, or anything else. They are simply examples. You could simply choose your equipment based on those presented here and you would do just fine. On the other extreme, you could use this information only as a starting point for your search of which item you will ultimately use.

Figure 2: Aluminum and Bamboo Steamers

First up, the steamer; the steamer is one of the few pieces of equipment that is not readily available from homebrew shops. They can usually be found in Oriental markets. One common steamer type is the bamboo steamer. Most others are aluminum or stainless steel. For the standard batch size that this book uses, a 12" diameter steamer with two levels makes a good and inexpensive choice.

Next up are the fermentation vessels. You need one for the moto and one for moromi. The one for moto can be pretty small, 2 to 4 quarts is just fine. The one for moromi should be much larger, about 5 gallons or 20 quarts is needed to ensure the foam from the fermentation does not overflow your container:

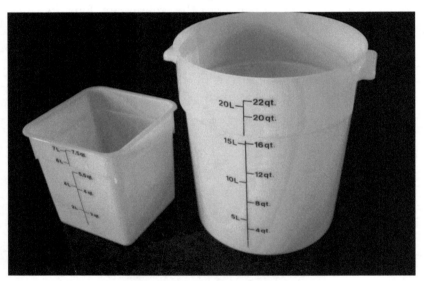

Figure 3: Food Grade Containers for fermenting

Next up is pressing, siphoning and transferring paraphernalia. Sakabukuro (bags to capture the kasu (lees)) are very helpful and just about the easiest way to strain a high percentage of the lees out of the sake. These can be used with or without a press. Brew shops carry mesh bags that fill this role. Paint filter bags available at hardware stores also work well. Be sure to thoroughly wash these before use to ensure your saké does not pick up any foul aromas.

Brewing Equipment

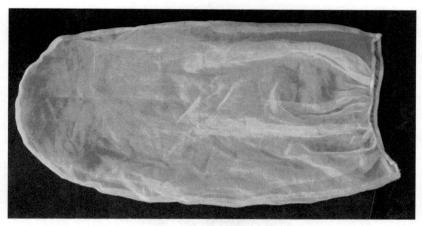

Figure 4: Strainer bad for pressing the moromi

As for a press, one example press type is a cheese press.

Figure 5: Cheese press for pressing the moromi

After straining and pressing you need vessels into which to put the saké that results. One gallon glass jugs work nicely for this. You should have 6 of these one gallon jugs; three to contain the saké from pressing and three for transferring the saké to after some of the lees have fallen out of solution. This transfer process from the first three jugs to the second three jugs is called racking. The goal here is to move the saké off the sediment for clearer saké. You might also want to have a funnel but these are common enough that I will not include examples.

As these jugs are the secondary fermentor, we will want to put an air lock on each.

Figure 6: A couple of 1 gallon jugs for conditioning

Every air lock needs a stopper. For those who have not seen one of these before, the air lock below is slid tightly into the center hole of the stopper below and the two together are fit tightly into the mouth of the jug. With water in the air lock the only gas that goes in or out will need to go under water first. The bit of ferment that is still continuing will be generating CO_2 and so as the pressure of the CO_2 rises in the jug it will force its way out by going through the water. As with the jugs, six stoppers and air locks are useful.

Figure 7: Air locks and stoppers

After the saké has conditioned in the secondary jug for a while, more of the lees will have settled to the bottom of the jug. By racking, that is transferring the saké from one vessel to a second vessel via siphoning; we can take just the clearest saké off the top. One of the easiest ways to do this is with the use of an auto-siphon. An auto siphon primes the racking cane by using a plunger action.

You can't use a racking cane without some tubing (hose) to carry the siphoned saké to the target vessel.

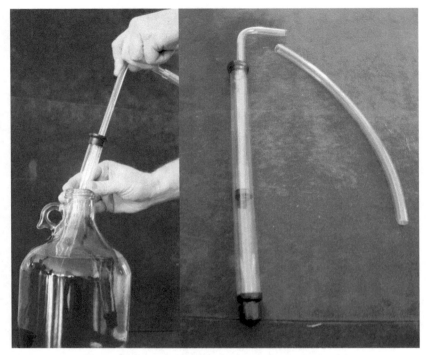

Figure 8: Auto siphon for racking (transferring) saké

Other pieces of equipment that you will need but should have around the house are:

- Measuring cups and spoons
- Bowls you can use to rinse, wash and soak the rice
- A long handle spoon for stirring the moto and moromi
- A Funnel mentioned above
- Pan or double boiler for pasteurization
- A thermometer with range from about 40°F – 160°F
- Vessels for the final saké to go into. These can be the jugs themselves but in most cases you will use other bottles. The main requirement is that you can seal them: screw cap, cork or crimped cap will all work fine.
- Cheese cloth, butter muslin cloth or some other loose weave cloth

Bottles with crimped caps, caps and a capper are an easy and secure way to go. However, if you choose this route you will need a capper like the following one.

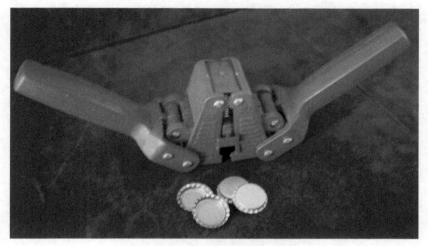

Figure 9: Bottle capper and caps

If you would like to measure any of the key characteristics of your saké you will need a few more items. These are not strictly needed but are nice to have especially if you plan to excel at brewing saké. The first of these, and the one that you can least do without is a hydrometer and hydrometer jar. The hydrometer is used to measure the specific gravity and Saké Meter Value (SMV) of the saké. The hydrometer can also be used in combination with a refractometer to evaluate the percentage alcohol by volume.

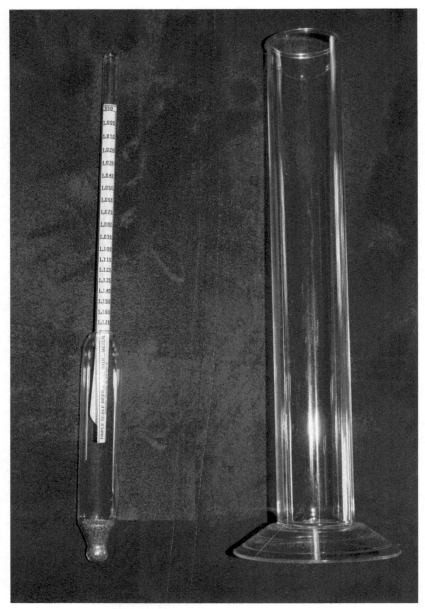
Figure 10: Hydrometer and hydrometer jar

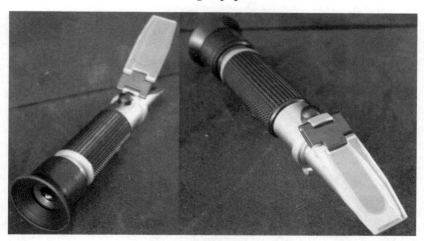

Figure 11: Refractometers

Another combination of items that can be used to measure the percent alcohol by volume, are a small beaker or flask in combination with the hydrometer.

Figure 12: Pyrex glassware

To measure the acidity or san-do a test kit like the one below will do the trick.

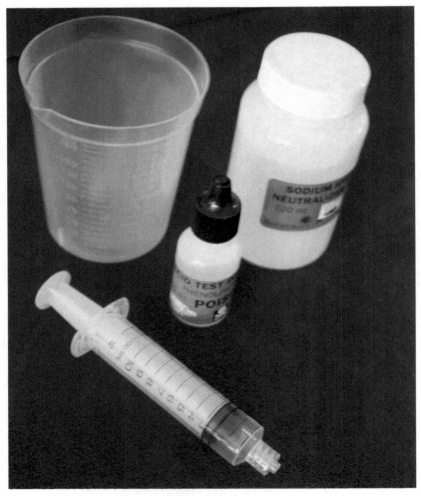

Figure 13: Wine acidity analysis kit

It is always good to have a good sanitizer. The one below is iodophor. It is mixed with water and takes only a minute to sanitize an object.

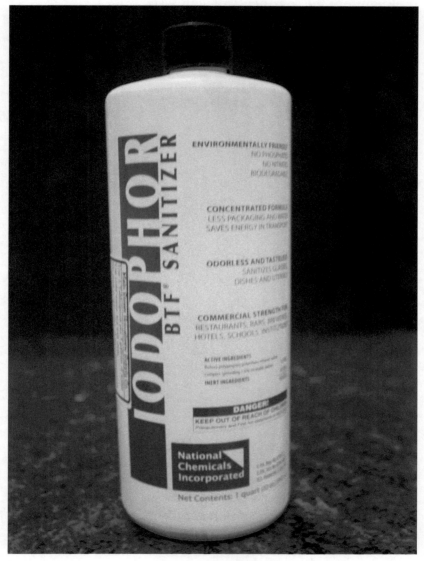

Figure 14: Iodophor

Temperature control of your ferment, all the way from moto through moromi and conditioning to bottling, is extremely important. So a control unit like the following Ranco model can really improve the consistency of your sake.

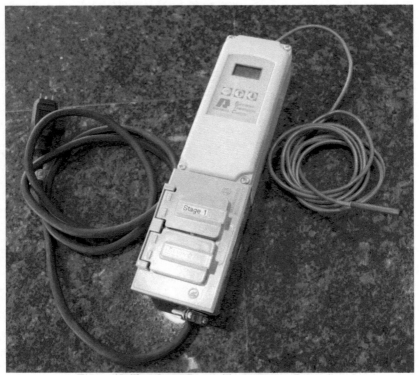

Figure 15: Two Stage Ranco Temperature Controller

This controller needs to be plugged into something that does the actual heating or cooling. For the ferment, a chest freezer works well. Small ones, about 7 cubic feet, don't take up much room and will hold two moromi at a time while larger ones will hold much more. For making koji, a small heater for keeping the incubation area warm, may be used with this same controller.

A koolatron insulated cooler is one example of a cooler that also has an element that can be set for either heating or cooling. When combined with the temperature controller it can hold the environment inside just where you want it to be.

Figure 16: Koolatron insulated cooler with heating and cooling

Finally the additional equipment used specifically for koji making is:

- Cloth with tight weave for wrapping
- Cooler to function as an incubator
- Thermometer (I like those with a probe that can be in the rice while the monitor is outside and easily visible)
- Temperature control, one of:
    o Controller with heater
    o Jars filled with hot water for temperature control
    o Heating pad

Well, that about covers the basics of the equipment.

Quick Start Saké Brewing

This quick start procedure is meant to help you get started as quickly as possible. It's a procedure you can use to make very good saké, now, without waiting to learn more. My hope is that, as you make your saké you will be pulled more and more into this unique drink and all its aspects, making your learning about the whys and what fors more exciting and magical.

This outline is specifically for use with rice milled to 60% of original (60% seimaibuai) and premade koji.

The big picture: The first task is to create the moto which is a yeast mash to grow up a strong population of yeast for the ferment. The moto lasts for one week in this procedure. Next is the buildup from the moto to the moromi or the yeast mash to the main ferment. This buildup comes in a three stage addition process over four days. Following the buildup is the main ferment that lasts about 20 days. This is followed by pressing to separate the saké from the lees and a series of rackings. The rackings transfer clear saké from containers with sediment to containers without sediment. This allows the saké to become more and more clear and more sediment free with each racking. Finally is the pasteurization and bottling, which completes the process. The total time from start to end is 88 days in this case. In the general case the time is closely tied to brewing temperature.

There is a tremendous amount of repetition in this process. For example, the same process used to create the moto is used for each of the three additions of the buildup. Racking is repeated several times and pasteurization is done twice. So, while the following outline is long, most of the work becomes comfortable and routine before you are done.

Before beginning there are a few things that you will need to decide. Some of the steps will need to be done about 12 hours apart. Some people arrange to do the first of these in the evening and the second in the morning. Others will choose to do the first in the morning and the second in the evening. In the following I will assume the morning and evening combination rather than the evening followed by morning version. However, you should feel free to shift the timing as needed to fit your schedule.

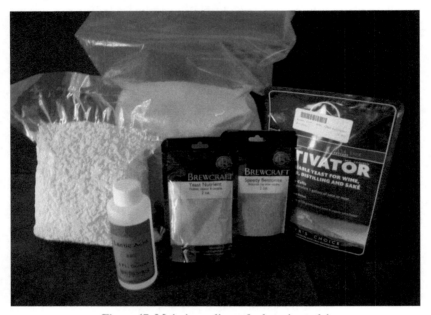

Figure 17: Main ingredients for brewing saké

To begin you will need the following ingredients:

- Rice milled to 60% seimaibuai – 10 lbs.
- Koji, fresh brewer's koji[1] – 2.5 lbs.
- Water – Just short of 2 US gallons or 30 cups total

---

[1] While not fresh brewers koji, Cold Mountain koji is readily available at oriental grocers across the country and will do the trick if you can't find fresh koji.

- Distilled, Reverse osmosis or very soft water – 2.5 cups
    - Iron free and Manganese free water – 27.5 cups
- Lactic acid 88% - 1 teaspoon
- Yeast nutrient – ½ teaspoon
- Epsom salts for magnesium sulfate – pinch
- Morton Salt Substitute for potassium chloride – 1 teaspoon
- Yeast, either Wyeast 3134 (#9) or White labs WLP705 (#7)

Wyeast package their yeast products in a soft pouch with an inner pouch that contains food and nutrients to give the yeast a good start. The intent is for the brewer to break open the inner packet several hours before use. This gives the yeast a head start and ensures they are healthy and ready to perform. To break open the inner packet the yeast packet is held in the palm of your hand and struck sharply, smacked, with the other hand.

One last note before getting started: you will need a sanitizer. If you choose iodophor, mix 1 tablespoon of iodophor per 5 US gallons of water to make a sanitizing solution. Use as called for.

Day 1 Morning – estimated task time 10 minutes:

The first thing we must do is prepare a few things; moto water, yeast and koji. This is done in the morning with the first rice steaming done in the evening. It could be done the night before the first rice steaming if you would rather.

Do:

- Take your yeast out of the refrigerator and leave on counter to warm (target temp:65°F-75°F)
- Place your koji into the refrigerator if it is not already there (you don't want it frozen).
- Put together your moto water. Combine and stir well:
    - 2.5 cups soft water (distilled or reverse osmosis water is best)
    - 1 teaspoon 88% lactic acid

- o 3/4th teaspoon yeast nutrient
- o Pinch of Epsom salts (Magnesium sulfate)
- o 1 teaspoon Morton's Salt Substitute (Potassium chloride)
- Put ½ cup of this water mixture in the refrigerator and cover
- Put 2 cups (the rest) on the counter next to the yeast and cover

That's it for the first bit of work. From here on, iron free tap water can be used in all cases.

Day 1 Evening – estimated task time 3.5 hours, beginning Moto:

This section has several distinct phases and one minor phase: broken up by steeping, draining and steaming.

Do phase 1:

- Smack your yeast pack if you have not already done so and are using Wyeast yeast (White labs yeast does not need to be smacked)
- Ready sanitizer
- Prepare rice
    - o 1.6 cups of rice
    - o Wash the rice in cold water till water is mostly clear
    - o Steep in cold water with 1" water over top of rice for 1 hour

Do phase 2:

- Sanitize the moto container
- Begin preparing the moto by combining (target temp: 70°F):
    - o 2 cups of moto water prepared in the morning
    - o Yeast
- Drain rice and place in a colander to drain for an hour

Do phase 3:

- Add 8/10th cup koji to moto water and yeast mixture
- Prepare steamer with cheese cloth liner
- Add drained rice to steamer
- Steam rice for 1 hour

Do phase 4:

- 30 minute check of the steaming rice to be sure you don't run out of water in the steamer.

Do phase 5:

- Cool rice after steaming – use the ½ cup moto water placed in refrigerator earlier in the morning
- Combine and mix well (target temp:72°F do not let it get to or above 90°F):
    - Moto starter from phase 2 and 3: moto water, yeast, koji
    - Freshly steamed and cooled rice
- Loosely cover with plastic wrap and place where it will not get too much light (target temp: 65°F-75°F)

Day 2-7 – estimated time 5 minutes

Do each day:

- Stir well twice a day with a sanitized spoon
- Target temp: 65°F-72°F

Day 8 – Day before starting the buildup to Moromi – estimated time 5+ minutes

Do:

- Stir the moto
- Begin lowering moto temperature, slowly, down to 60°F

Day 9 Morning – estimated time 10 minutes

The moto should now be at about 60°F.

Do:

- Mix with Moto:
    o 1.5 cups koji
    o 1.5 cups water (iron free tap water will be fine at this stage)
- Place 1.25 cups water into the refrigerator to use in the evening

Day 9 Evening – estimated time 3.5 hours

Hatsuzoe, the first addition.

This section has several distinct phases: broken up by steeping, draining and steaming. This is mostly the same as day 2 with a different amount of rice and without the yeast.

Do phase 1:

- Start cooling the moto to 50°F
- Prepare rice
    o 2.5 cups of rice
    o Wash the rice in cold water till water is mostly clear
    o Steep in cold water with 1" water over top of rice for 1 hour

Do phase 2:

- Drain rice and place in a colander to drain for an hour

Do phase 3:

- Prepare steamer with cheese cloth liner
- Add drained rice to steamer
- Steam rice for 1 hour

Do phase 4:

- 30 minute check of the steaming rice to be sure you don't run out of water in the steamer.

Do phase 5:

- Ready sanitizer
- Sanitize the large 5 to 7 gallon fermentor
- Cool rice after steaming – use 1.25 cups water placed in refrigerator in the morning
- Place steamed and cooled rice into the fermentor
- Mix the moto with the rice in the fermentor
- Loosely cover with plastic wrap and place where it will not get too much light (target temp: 55°F)

Do for next 48 hours at 12 hour intervals:

- Stir the ferment for 5 minutes

The day after first addition, Hatsuzoe, (that is day 10) is Odori, the dancing ferment.

Day 11 Morning – estimated time 10 minutes

The ferment should now be about 55°F to 60°F.

Do:

- Mix with Moto:
    - 2.25 cups koji
    - 4.5 cups water
- Place 4.25 cups water into the refrigerator to use in the evening

Day 11 Evening – estimated time 3.5 hours

Nakazoe, the middle addition begins 48 hours after the first addition, Hatsuzoe.

This section has several distinct phases: broken up by steeping, draining and steaming. This is mostly the same as day 8 with a different amount of rice, koji and water.

Do phase 1:

- Start cooling the ferment to 50°F
- Prepare rice
    - 6 cups of rice
    - Wash the rice in cold water till water is mostly clear
    - Steep in cold water with 1" water over top of rice for 1 hour

Do phase 2:

- Drain rice and place in a colander to drain for an hour

Do phase 3:

- Prepare steamer with cheese cloth liner
- Add drained rice to steamer
- Steam rice for 1 hour

Do phase 4:

- 30 minute check of the steaming rice to be sure you don't run out of water in the steamer.

Do phase 5:

- Cool rice after steaming – using 4.25 cups water prepared earlier in the morning and placed in refrigerator
- Place steamed and cooled rice into the fermentor
- Mix well in the fermentor
- Loosely cover the fermentor with plastic wrap and place somewhere out of the light where it will cool (target temp: 50°F)

Day 12 Morning – estimated time 10 minutes

- Mix with ferment:
    - 3.5 cups koji
    - 10 cups water
- Place 6 cups water into the refrigerator to use in the evening

Day 12 Evening – estimated time 3.5 hours

Tomezoe, the last addition in the buildup of the Moromi, begins 24 hours after Nakazoe.

This section has several distinct phases: broken up by steeping, draining and steaming. This is mostly the same as day 11 with a different amount of rice, koji and water.

Do phase 0:

- Stir the ferment

Do phase 1:

- Ferment should be close to 50°F
- Prepare rice
    - 10 cups of rice
    - Wash the rice in cold water till water is mostly clear
    - Steep in cold water with 1" water over top of rice for 1 hour

Do phase 2:

- Drain rice and place in a colander to drain for an hour

Do phase 3:

- Prepare steamer with cheese cloth liner
- Add drained rice to steamer
- Steam rice for 1 hour

Do phase 4:

- 30 minute check of the steaming rice to be sure you don't run out of water in the steamer.

Do phase 5:

- Cool rice after steaming – use 6 cups water prepared earlier in the day and placed in refrigerator
- Place steamed, cooled rice into the fermentor
- Mix ferment well
- Loosely cover fermentor with plastic wrap and place where it will not get too much light (target temp: 50°F)

Do for next 2 days at 12 hour intervals:

- Stir the ferment

Day 15 through 31 – relax but monitor the temperature to ensure the ferment goes well.

Day 32 – estimated time 1.5 hours

Time to press! We must separate the saké from the lees to start to clarify our saké. At this stage we also rack to the secondary fermentor (glass jugs).

Do phase 1:

- Prepare the sanitizer solution
- Sanitize 3 glass 1 gallon jugs
- Sanitize 3 air locks with stoppers
- Sanitize a container for collecting saké from the pressing
- Sanitize a funnel
- Prepare the cloth or bag for holding the moromi while pressing
- Line the container for collecting your saké with the cloth or bag for holding the moromi

Do phase 2:

- Transfer a portion of the moromi into the cloth or bag and begin to squeeze the saké through to the container, as needed, transfer the saké into a jug
- Repeat until all the moromi has been pressed and the saké is in the 3 jugs
- Place jugs where they will not get too much light (target temp: 50°F)

Do phase 3 (optional)

- Prepare an Hydrometer to measure the specific gravity
- Place sample in the Hydrometer jar and float the Hydrometer in the sample
- Read and record the specific gravity. Expect it to be around 1.010 to 1.002 depending on clarity.

The saké in the jugs will still be quite milky in most cases but should not have any rice mixed in.

Day 33 to 43 – Let the saké rest

Day 44 – estimated time 0.5 hours

Transfer saké off lees into new jugs (i.e., rack saké to new jugs). The idea is to move the clear saké off the lees that have sunk to the bottom without stirring them up and mixing them with the clear saké.

Do:

- Sanitize 3 new glass 1 gallon jugs, optionally air locks
- Decant or siphon the clear saké into the new glass jugs
- Fill new jugs up to within a few inches of the top
- Place jugs where it will not get too much light (target temp: 50°F)

Day 45 to 53 – Let the saké rest

Day 54 – estimated time 0.5 hours

Rack again. Transfer saké off lees into new jugs. The idea is to move the clear saké off the lees that have sunk to the bottom again without stirring them up and mixing them with the clear saké.

Do:

- Sanitize 3 new glass 1 gallon jugs, air locks and stoppers
- Decant or siphon the clear saké into the new glass jugs
- Fill new jugs up to within a few inches of the top
- Place jugs where they will not get too much light (target temp: 50°F)

Day 55 to 67 – Let the saké rest

Day 68 – estimated time 2.0 hours

Time to rack and pasteurize.

Do phase 1:

- Sanitize 3 new glass containers, air locks and stoppers
- Rack the clear saké off the lees and into the new jugs

The saké and lees left may be the correct consistency for nigori. If you choose, you can pasteurize this separately as nigori.

Do phase 2:

- Prepare a double boiler or water bath that can hold the jugs of saké for pasteurization, likely one jug at a time
- Place the jug in the water bath while the water is cool
- Bring the water bath up in temperature tracking the temperature of the saké (target 140°F to 150°F)
- Remove saké from bath when it reaches temperature and let cool to room temperature
- Place airlock on jug and return to cool place (target temp. 45°F to 50°F)

Day 69 to 87 – Let saké rest

Day 88 – estimated time 3.0 hours

Time to rack, pasteurize and bottle.

Do phase 1:

- Sanitize 3 new glass containers
- Rack the clear saké off the lees and into the sanitized containers

The saké and lees left may be the correct consistency for nigori. As before, if you choose, you can pasteurize this separately as nigori.

Do phase 2 (optional):

- Prepare an Hydrometer to measure the specific gravity
- Place sample in the Hydrometer jar and float the Hydrometer in the sample
- Read and record the specific gravity. Expect it to be around 0.998 to 0.990 depending on clarity.

Do phase 3 (optional) amelioration:

- We want to have an SMV of about +5 which is a specific gravity of 0.996
- Assume specific gravity from phase 2 is X
- To raise the specific gravity measured in phase 2 to 0.996 it takes 9.5 g of table sugar per specific gravity point per gallon
    - Add Z grams = (0.996 - X) * 1000 * Y gallons * 9.5
- Dissolve Z grams of table sugar in saké and mix in well

Do phase 4:

- Sanitize a funnel and bottles with caps
- Fill bottles with saké from the jugs

Do phase 5:

- Prepare a double boiler or water bath on the stove that can hold the bottles of saké for pasteurization
- Place the bottles in the water bath while the water is cool
- Bring the water bath up in temperature tracking the temperature of the saké (target 140°F to 150°F)
- Remove saké bottles from bath when it reaches 140°F
- Cap bottle when saké is no longer hot

Following this procedure will produce saké that is clear, dry and very high quality.

Rice – Kome (米)

OK, so what about rice? Isn't it all the same? Well, I guess there is brown rice and white rice. Isn't this all there is to it? No, it's not, there's much more. While we are interested in saké rice, I will cover some basic background and history to build a foundation we can use to better understand rice, its differences, and what is important for making saké.

The scientific name for the species we call rice is Oryza Sativa. Within this species are three subspecies: Japonica (usually short-grain rice), Indica (long-grain rice) and Javanica (usually medium-grain rice). Javanica is now known as Tropical Japonica. While Japonica seems to imply that it originates in Japan this is not the case. In fact, it appears that the origin is China.

The earliest evidence for rice being eaten as a regular source of food is around 10000 to 9000 BC in the Yangtze River valley of China. By 8000 to 7000 BC this rice had been domesticated. During the period 3000 to 2000 BC rice cultivation spread from china throughout Southeast Asia and westward to India. Rice made it to Japan somewhere between 3500 and 1200 BC. However intensive wet paddy agriculture did not arrive in Japan until circa 300 BC.

One of the oldest rice strains used for making saké is Omachi. It is a pure rice strain discovered in 1859 in western Okayama Prefecture and has been continually grown until now. Omachi was, in the Meiji period, a shokumai or rice for eating but is no longer used for food. While Omachi is an excellent rice for high quality saké it is hard to grow being very tall. Despite this it is the second most popular rice for making high grade ginjo and daiginjo. One of its prodigies is Gohyakumangoku which is the highest volume saké rice in Japan.

Gohyakumangoku Rice produces nicely dry and fragrant saké. The name literally means five million bags of rice. Mainly used for futsu shu, honjozo, junmai and ginjo it is the most popular brewing rice in Japan. This rice tends to produce very dry, light and tart style saké. While Gohyakumangoku is the overall champion, Yamadanishiki is the champion for ginjo and daiginjo saké.

Yamadanishiki is the crowned king of saké rice. Yamadanishiki is famous for its use in high quality saké. It is particularly desired by saké brewers for its ability to absorb water and dissolve easily. The shinpaku, that is the starchy center of the rice, dissolves easily leaving the outer shell. Yamadanishiki has much less protein and fat than most rice. Less protein makes the taste of saké crisp and light, and less fat makes saké more flavorful. Yamadanishiki was bred in 1923 from Yamadaho of Hyogo Prefecture and Tankan Wataribune of Ibaragi Prefecture. However, it wasn't named until 1936.

Wataribune from Ibaraki prefecture, like Omachi, is a pure rice strain. It produces wonderful saké. It is a parent of Yamadanishiki and was a major contributor to California rice and hence Australia's rice as well. However, it fell out of use until recently when Fuchu Homare Brewery brought it back into production in 1988. Their first saké made from this reintroduced rice was brewed in 1990.

Sakamai or Saké Rice is only a small part of the story for rice in Japan. Shokumai or eating rice is much more important in terms of the general economy. However given our focus here I will only mention two cultivars. Koshihikari: This rice brings the highest prices for rice in Japan because of its excellent flavor and properties. Hitomebore was created by combining Koshihikari with another Japanese rice variety. Hitomebore literally means "falling in love with a person at first glance." I mention these two mostly because we will see them again below.

It wasn't until 1686 that rice made it to North America, South Carolina, from Madagascar. This began the first cultivation of rice in North America. The predominant strain of rice was from Madagascar and was known as "Carolina White." Soon after, "Carolina Gold" came on to the scene and dominated the market. It was most likely a selection from Carolina White but we do not know for sure. Rice cultivation continued to spread in the southeast. Within 23 years, Charleston had become wealthy in large part because of the rice trade. Little change occurred for the next 200 years.

South Carolina and Georgia produced more than 90% of the rice produced in the US by 1850. By 1890, just 40 years later, rice production in South Carolina and Georgia had ceased as cultivation moved westward. The next documented rice introduction occurred with Honduras, a long grain rice. Neither Carolina Gold nor Honduras had good milling qualities with breakage levels of 40% to 60%. Resulting profits were much lower than they should be because of the high degree of breakage during milling. This set the stage for a more suitable rice to be introduced.

Seaman A. Knapp, commissioned by a newly formed arm of the US government, traveled to Japan in 1898 to locate more suitable rice for Louisiana. By this time the Atlantic coast was no longer producing significant amounts of rice. Knapp returned with a Japanese rice, Kiushu, he felt would be best suited for Louisiana. Tested in the 1899 season, Kiushu proved to be vastly superior to both Carolina Gold and Honduras in reducing breakage loss, breakage dropped to between 14% to 18%, and increased overall yields by more than 25%.

As a result, several hundred tons of Kiushu seed were imported enabling Kiushu to become Louisiana's leading variety. Kiushu also spread to Texas. In fact Louisiana and Texas had more than half their acreage of rice planted with Kiushu by 1907. Knapp made a second, more extensive trip and brought back many more varieties, including Chinriki and Wataribune, to be tested. These varieties were very important in taking Louisiana and Texas from producing 100,000,000 pounds of rice in 1896 to over 687,000,000 pounds in 1911, more than a 6 fold increase.

Crowley, Louisiana in 1905 took over the work Knapp had been doing. This work had started near Manchester, Louisiana and then moved to a farm near North Galveston, Texas before finding its final rest at Crowley. The Kiushu and Chinriki rice varieties were the best available varieties until Salmon Lusk "Sol" Wright introduced his Blue Rose in 1907 and Early Prolific soon after. Wright developed Blue Rose in an attempt to control red rice which devalued the rice crop. He strongly believed that a domestic variety needed to be bred. By 1934 close to 75% of the rice grown in the US were varieties developed by Wright.

The original stock from which Blue Rose and Early Prolific were derived is unclear to me. Both are tropical Japonica medium grain while the varieties Knapp brought from Japan are temperate Japonica. So, it does not seem like they would have been derived from the Japanese lines. Both Carolina Gold and Honduras are tropical Japonica.

Long grain varieties were tested on Onion Island in the San Joaquin River near Stockton, California in the early 1890s but with no success. Then, in 1906, in the San Joaquin Valley, William W. Mackie was experimenting with a short-grain Japanese cultivar brought in from Hawaii. Finding success, Mackie went to Louisiana and Texas to learn more about rice culture. In 1908 Mackie was able to arrange another trial with short grain rice. This time he used Kiushu that he obtained from Crowley, Louisiana and in a second attempt found success with a yield of 3000 pounds per acre.

With the gold rush in California came Chinese immigrants and rice. The first commercial production began in 1912 in Butte County, California. Early production used a cultivar known as "Chinese" from China and soon after this, Early Wataribune from Japan. A selection from Chinese was named Colusa, released in 1917. Coloro, a selection from Wataribune, was released in 1921. The cultivars Chinese and Wataribune are both short-grain as are the selections from them. Short-grain cultivars, primarily Colusa and Coloro, were the primary cultivars in California until the 1960s. These grains had low amylose content and a low gelatinization temperature.

By 1941 Louisiana had nine principal kinds of rice. They included: Blue Rose, Early Prolific, Fortuna, Rexora, Lady Wright, Edith,

Rice – Kome (米)

Nira, Japanese and Shoemed. Soon after this, Calrose was created in California.

Calrose was created by crossing Coloro with Calady[2] which produced a medium-grain rice cultivar. With its release in 1948, it and its prodigy shifted California's production away from short-grain rice to medium-grain. Calrose remained in production through the end of the 1970s. A semi-dwarf cultivar from Calrose was created by inducing the mutation through gamma radiation of Calrose seeds. It stands 25% shorter than Calrose. This semi-dwarf mutant of Calrose was named Calrose 76 and it took over where Calrose itself left off.

Calrose 76 amylose content is about 18%, and so the rice tends to be a little on the softer side and the kernels cling together. Gelatinization temperature is about 60 degree centigrade; protein tends to average about 6.5%

Today, the six counties north of Sacramento produce the second largest rice crop in the US after Arkansas. However, for us, the main point of interest is that this area grows short grain and median grain japonica rice varieties. This includes the cultivar Calrose, Calrose 76 and their prodigy which make up about 85% of California's crop.

There are at least three japonica short grained rice varieties grown in California: Koshihikari, Hitomebore and Akita Komachi. Koshihikari was created in 1956 by crossing two strains of Nourin No. 1 and Nourin No. 22 at the Fukui Prefecture Agricultural Research Facility. Hitomebore was created in 1991 by crossing Koshihikari with another Japanese variety at Miyagi Prefectural Furukawa Agricultural Experiment Station. Akita Komachi has also been derived from Koshihikari.

Australia began cultivation of California varieties in New South Wales in the 1920s. Rice cultivation had been tried without success

---

[2] Calady, a medium grained rice, was selected from a cross between Coloro, a short grain rice, and Lady Wright, a long grained variety.

for many years in the north of Australia. However within the Murray-Darling Basin of New South Wales the heavy soil with cheap water for irrigation, provided the needed environment that could not be found in the north. Once Calrose was developed it became the backbone of the Australian rice industry. Calrose 76 also migrated to Australia and was the source of nine derivative semi-dwarf varieties specific to Australia.

So what does all this mean for us? Japanese saké brewers use only short grain rice, Japonica, for saké. Rice suitable for brewing saké is larger than average with a larger starch core (Shinpaku), as well as less protein and fat. These properties help produce the higher millability of the short grain rice. Calrose is commonly available, inexpensive and regularly used by home saké brewers. However, it is a medium grained rice with less shinpaku than the short grained varieties. Koshihikari, Hitomebore and Akita Komachi, while more expensive, are all short grained and are worth giving a try in your saké brewing.

Make up of a rice kernel

Brewing refined saké requires that we remove many layers of the rice, but why? Well before we get to that, let's look at what these layers are.

The outer most layer of freshly harvested rice is the chaff. This is a layer that protects the inner seed of the grain. In the following chart, the chaff is the outer most layer. A picture of rice chaff that has been removed from the grain is also shown below. The chaff is on the top left of figure 19.

Once the chaff has been removed we are left with brown rice. Brown rice appears brown because of the bran outer layer. This bran outer layer contains vitamins, dietary minerals, oils, fatty acids, dietary fibers, starch and protein. The vitamins include B1, B3, B12 and a form of E in addition to the minerals magnesium and iron.

Rice – Kome (米)

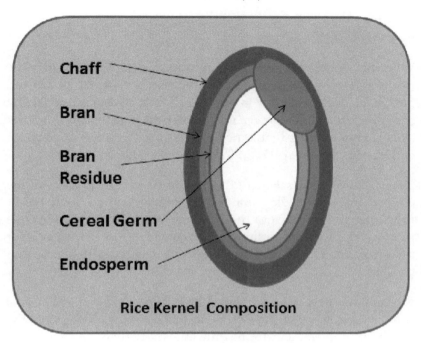

Figure 18: Makeup of a rice kernel

Brown rice is about 70-75% starch. Starch is by far the most abundant component of rice. Rice starch is made up of two types of starch, amylose and amylopectin. High amylose rice contains 25% to 30% of its starch being amylose and is dry and fluffy after cooking. Medium amylose rice contains from 15% to 25% amylose which produces tender and slightly cohesive cooked rice. Low amylose rice contains 10% to 15% amylose and becomes soft and tender but a little sticky when cooked. Finally, glutinous or waxy rice has the lowest amylose, containing less than 2% amylose and is very sticky when cooked. Low to medium amylose is best for saké brewing.

The next most abundant component of brown rice is protein at about 7-8%. Protein is more prevalent in the outer layers of the grain. Fats make up about 2%. Both saturated and unsaturated fatty acids are present with the center having more saturated fatty acids while the outer layers have more unsaturated fatty acids. Ash makes up about 1% of the grain and includes: potassium, phosphorus, magnesium, and calcium.

While brown rice is much more nutritious than the standard white rice it also goes rancid much more quickly because of its oils and fatty acids that are mostly in the bran. The bran, bran residual and germ are removed through a milling process to produce white rice. This is your standard table rice processing which leaves only the endosperm, the inner 93 to 90% of the rice kernel.

Special saké rice (sakemai) has an area in the center of the endosperm that is called shinpaku. Shinpaku is the starchy ball at the center and is really just more prevalent in saké rice than in table rice. The more prevalent the shinpaku the more suited the rice is for saké making. This is, in part, due to its synergy with the milling process.

Rice milling for saké goes beyond the milling of table rice. The goal is to remove more of the fatty acids and proteins leaving only the starchy center. In the extreme only little more than the shinpaku is left. The more of the outer layer that is removed the more refined the saké. Rice from brown to highly milled is shown in the following picture. Milling is graded using the seimaibuai scale. This is the percentage of rice left after milling. Using this scale, saké is graded roughly as follows:

- 90% to 70% seimaibuai is Futsu-shu
- 70% to 60% seimaibuai is Junmai-shu[3] or Honjozo-shu
- 60% to 50% seimaibuai is Junmai Ginjo-shu or Ginjo-shu
- 50% and below seimaibuai is Junmai Daiginjo-shu or Daiginjo-shu

---

[3] Prior to Jan. 1, 2004, Junmai-shu needed a seimaibuai of 70% or lower. Now, the seimaibuai, whatever it is, must be printed on the label while following the rest of the junmai-shu restrictions to be labeled as Junmai-shu.

Rice – Kome (米)

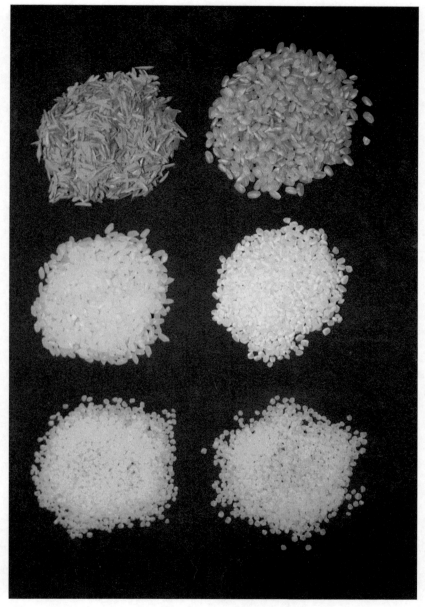

Figure 19: Samples of rice chaff and brown rice followed by increasing levels of milled rice

The difference between the "Junmai" and the other alternative above (e.g., Honjozo or Ginjo) is that the later has some brewers alcohol added while the former does not. Futsu-shu is also more relaxed about additions whereas the higher grade sakés can have no other ingredients other than rice, koji, water, and alcohol in the non-junmai case. Despite these ranges some brewers will sell a saké that falls in, say, the daiginjo range as ginjo because they do not feel it represents their breweries standards for daiginjo. So you can think of the classification as setting the minimum standards.

Why do saké brewers want to remove the outer layers of rice? Well, bran and its oils (10-15% of the bran), the fatty acids (the unsaturated ones) and proteins do not interact well with the yeast to produce desirable flavors and aromas. So, by removing the outer layers that contain the highest concentration of these unwanted components, we can brew better, more refined, saké. In addition, saké produced from milled rice is more stable because the unstable oils and fatty acids have been removed.

Koji (麹)

The most mysterious ingredient used to make saké is koji. What is it? Why is it so important? What does it contribute to saké? Well, these are all important questions we will address here. Koji is a general term that is almost always used as a specific term by those talking about saké. In the general case koji is some kind of substrate with some kind of mold growing on it. How's that for a technical description? Koji that is used for making saké is, in most cases, yellow koji consisting of Aspergillus Oryzae growing on milled rice.

Yellow koji is also used for making Shochu, a distilled beverage, but has been mostly replaced by other forms of mold and substrate. The two most common molds that are currently used for koji in the production of shochu are Aspergillus Kawachi (white) and Aspergillus Awamori (black). In the general case, the substrates also vary quite a bit. Substrates of buckwheat, sweet potato, barley and rice are common. Rice is always the substrate used for saké.

One other koji, Beni Koji, is worth mentioning. Beni Koji is better known as red yeast rice, which is Monascus purpureus mold growing on rice as the substrate.

The general term for the mold spores is koji-kin or tane-koji but is often called Moyashi by brewers because of its sprout like characteristics at the micro level. Spores from any of the above molds can go by any of these names.

I mention that general case so that your thinking about koji will remain somewhat open. However, from this point on, I will limit my discussion to the more specific case of koji used in the brewing of saké.

Some Koji History

Koji has been used in the orient for two to three thousand years. Its use on a substrate of rice, soybean and wheat bran seems to have originated in China. Use of koji migrated to Japan in the Yayoi period around the change in the western calendar from BC to AD. Somewhere in the Heian and Muromachi period, between the thirteenth and the fifteenth centuries AD, koji became commercially available.

This was, in part, possible because of the use of hardwood leaf ash. The leaves were burned in an environment with limited oxygen to produce an ash/charcoal that was protective for the koji-kin. Koji-kin came packed, layered, in boxes with a layer of koji-kin then ash and repeated. The use of ash in packing to preserve the koji-kin led to the discovery that adding the ash directly to steamed rice produced more consistent koji production. We now know the alkaline environment from the ash prevents other microorganisms from getting a foothold and that the minerals in the ash help mold growth.

Moyashi or fermentation starter suppliers, two of them, were established in the Muromachi period about 1400AD. The Koji-za did not license more than these two prior to 1700AD. Currently, there seems to be about five or six such producers.

Koji Production

To begin a batch of saké, one of the first things that needs to be done is to make koji. Making koji is called seigiku and consists of preparing rice, inoculating the rice and cultivating the mold. The most common procedure is to steam the rice to produce an even consistency for the mold mycelium to grow into the center and around the rice. After steaming, the rice is cooled to a good

Koji (麹)

temperature for inoculation with koji-kin (below 115°F). Koji-kin is sprinkled over and thoroughly mix with the prepared rice. After inoculation the rice is wrapped up to keep it warm and moist for close to 24 hours. Once this first half of the growth is passed the mycelia start to become visible on the rice. During the second half of the time the rice koji is mixed every couple of hours to keep it from overheating. The following pictures illustrate what koji looks like when it is done and ready for making saké.

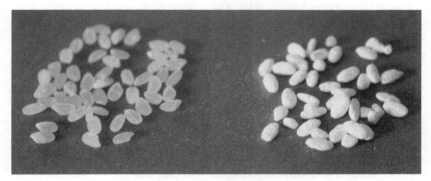

Figure 20: Rice (Left) and Koji (Right)

Figure 21: Fresh Brewer's Koji

OK, this is all well and good but why is koji important for brewing saké and what does it contribute? Well, koji is important because it contributes enzymes that are needed to break down rice starch into sugar and sugar is just what yeast need to produce ethanol and carbon dioxide. In a sense the koji and yeast are setting up a production line for the manufacturer of ethanol from starch. To be sure much more is created in this process including proteins, amino acids and the volatile compounds like alcohols and phenols which all combine to make up saké. For example some of the enzymes produced by koji act on proteins rather than starch and transform them into their amino acid constituents.

Before we go too far, what is an enzyme? An enzyme is a protein that acts as a catalyst. That is, a protein that performs some type of function that increases the rates of reactions. What enzymes are produced by koji? Well, koji produce many enzymes. A few of the known enzymes koji produce are:

- Alpha-amylase – breaks polysaccharides (starches) at random location
- Beta-amylase – snips off two glucose units (maltose) at a time– Not all strains of Aspergillus Oryzae produce beta-amylase
- Gamma-amylase – snips off a single glucose unit (glucose) at a time from polysaccharides
- Protease's – breaks proteins into smaller parts (amino acids, peptides)
- Peptidases – breaks up polypeptides (chains of amino acids)
- Sulfatases – breaks down sulphate esters to remove sulphates from substrates

In terms of the conversion of rice starch into sugar the alpha, beta and gamma-amylase are the enzymes to watch. They each work on the 1-4 link between glucose or maltose molecules. What? What is the 1-4 link between glucose molecules? Hmm. A little more background is needed.

Koji (麹)

Sugar and Starch

Glucose is the simplest (tied with fructose) sugar molecule. Both glucose and fructose have the same formula $C_6H_{12}O_6$ but have different ring structures. In the glucose diagram below the C at the right most edge is the first connection point (1). These points are counted moving in a clockwise manner through the Cs in the ring until the fifth C (5) with the sixth C hanging off the top (6). The ring is formed by the first (1) and fifth (5) connecting through an oxygen atom. Fructose is similar but has its second and fifth points connected through an oxygen atom to form the ring. This leaves both the first and sixth Cs hanging free. When two glucose molecules are joined to make a maltose molecule the first (1) position of one of the glucose is connected to the forth (4) position of the other glucose as shown in the maltose diagram. It is this (1-4) bond that is the main connection the amylase enzymes pull apart.

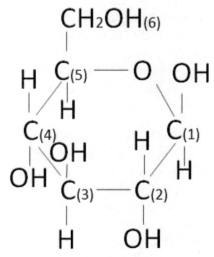

Figure 22: Glucose Molecule

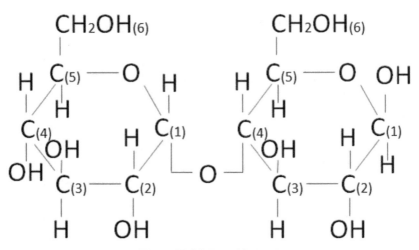

Figure 23: Maltose Molecule

Now for the most part starches are long chains of sugars. Actually the shortest chains are sugars, those a little longer are dextrins and those longer still are starches. It is a little more complicated in that not all these structures are strait chains without branching. Amylose is non-branched or strait chains of starch while Amylopectin is branched or non-strait chains of starch. In amylopectin the branches are formed with 1-6 links that occur about every 25 glucose molecules. Non-fermentable sugars and dextrins make up much of the mouth feel of a drink.

OK, now that we have a better understanding of the makeup of starch we can look at the difference in the way that alpha, beta and gamma amylase works as compared to each other. Gamma amylase mostly works by pulling a single glucose off the end of a polysaccharide chain by breaking the 1-4 link. However it may also break other links like the 1-6 links. Beta amylase always works from one end of the starch, dextrin or sugar and pulls off one maltose molecule at a time (i.e., two glucose) by breaking the 1-4 link. Yeast has no trouble processing either glucose or maltose sugar. Alpha amylase, in contrast, chooses a random 1-4 link to separate. This process results in two chains of arbitrary size; much of the time the resulting chains are not sugar and cannot be processed by yeast.

Even when one, the other or both are sugars, many types of yeast have a hard time with the more complex sugars.

In addition, time, temperature and pH are all important in the processes of converting starches. Each of the amylase has its own optimal range of temperature and pH that provide the most rapid and efficient environment with which to work. Alpha amylase operates best at 5.5 pH and beta amylase is optimal at 5.0 pH while gamma amylase works best around 3.0 pH. Alpha amylase performs best at a temperature of 158°F while beta amylase works best at a temperature of 140°F.

The optimal enzymatic temperatures are much higher than those we like to use for fermentation. At fermentation temperatures the enzyme activity will slow to a crawl. Also, a saké ferment has a low pH of around 3.0 which will favor gamma amylase while greatly reducing the activity of alpha and beta amylase. The result of using koji in saké fermentation is that the primary enzyme working to produce sugar for the yeast is gamma amylase. Gamma amylase produces sugar in a nice slow fashion that provides the yeast with sugar at a rate that the yeast can keep up with without becoming overly stressed.

Protein, peptides and amino acids

Now what about enzymes that work on protein? Well, in many ways they are similar to the enzymes we have just been considering. They all work by breaking proteins apart at their peptide bond. Again a little background will be helpful.

Proteins are very complex but for the most part, in this discussion, we will be able to ignore this fact because of a common feature of all amino acids. The formula for an amino acid is shown in the following figure. This figure shows two separate peptides in the first row. By combining the OH from the left peptide and the H from the right peptide we get a molecule of water and can then connect the remaining components to form the peptide bond at the C-N nodes; shown in the second row.

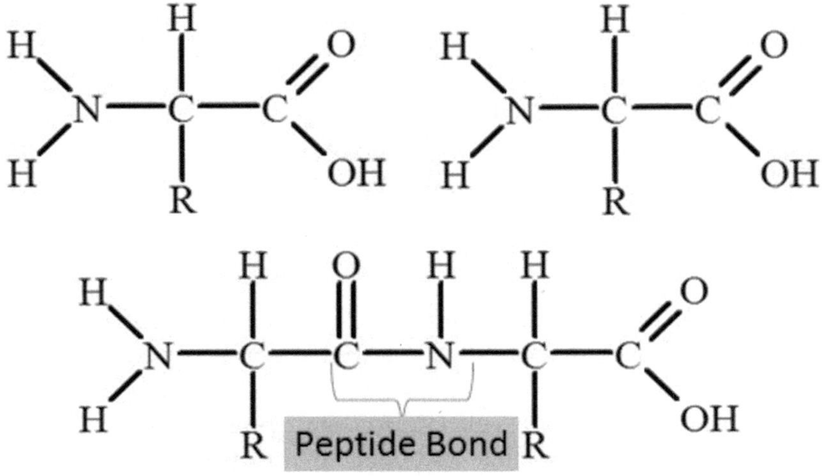

Figure 24: Peptide Bond

The R in the figure represents the remainder of the protein string. These strings, Rs, can be very complex in their own right. Combining these with several or even many other proteins, all connected through peptide bonds, can create extremely large and complex proteins. However, while R is often complex it can also be quite simple. For example the R in the amino acid glycin, CH_2NH_2COOH, is a single H in $CHRNH_2 COOH$. We will make use of this fact later in the method for measuring the amount of amino acid in saké.

As the enzymes work by pulling apart the peptide bond you might think that all of the enzymes work in the same way. They do not. As with the amylase enzymes, the enzymes that work on proteins attach to the protein or peptide in different ways. They connect like a lock and key with the enzyme taking hold of only those proteins that fit in the lock. For example, the peptidases only work on smaller proteins while the protease works on large proteins.

While we try to eliminate most of the proteins from our rice by milling to higher levels we can't get rid of them all. Also, koji produces proteins. Yes, that's right! While we are milling the rice to remove fatty acids and proteins the koji is adding them. And, in fact, they are not all bad. However, we do not want any large proteins, only those that are medium to small. Large proteins cannot be used by the yeast as they can use nothing more complex than amino acids to build up their cell walls. In addition large proteins contribute to chill haze. On the other hand medium to small proteins add a fuller body and mouth feel. All this emphasizes the need for the enzymes to break down the proteins.

Aroma, not the least for koji

The aroma of a fresh batch of koji is often described as being chestnut like. This aroma becomes noticeable by 20 hours into the koji production process, not strong but definitely there. As the time goes by the aroma strengthens. So what is making this aroma?

It seems, based on many studies[4] that the aroma is coming from a combination of the phenol phenylacetaldehyde, and the alcohols 1-octen-3-ol and 1-octen-3-one. Production of phenylacetaldehyde seems to stop at around 40 hours into the process while the production of 1-octen-3-ol and 1-octen-3-one continues and can even double their concentration during the final stages of koji production (hours 44-50). However, as 1-octen-3-ol and 1-octen-3-

---

4 Three of the studies are:

1. GC-Olfactometry analysis of the aroma components in saké koji. by Takahashi Mie et. al., in the Journal of the Brewing Society of Japan
2. Change in the aroma of saké koji during koji-making by Takahashi et. al, in Journal of the Brewing Society of Japan (May 2007) Analysis of Volatile Compounds in Shochu Koji, Saké Koji
3. Steamed Rice by Gas Chromatography-Mass Spectrometry by Yumiko Yoshizaki et. al., J. Inst. Brew. 116(1), 49–55, 2010

one concentrations overwhelm those of phenylacetaldehyde a more mushroom like aroma becomes noticeable. Individually phenylacetaldehyde and 1-octen-3-one have a rose like and a mushroom like aroma respectively.

As mycelia grow they produce linoleic acid. From linoleic acid 1-octen-3-ol is created and 1-octen-3-one is an enzymatic oxidation of 1-octen-3-ol. So the more mycelia growth there is the more 1-octen-3-ol and 1-octen-3-one there will be. One study found 5 novel compounds that are important to koji aroma:

Compound	Aroma
1-octen-3-one	Mushroom-like
2-methyl-2-hepten-6-one	Nut-like
methional	Potato-like
phenylacetaldehyde	Rose-like
(Z)-1, 5-octadien-3-one	Geranium-like
isobutyraldehyde	
isovaleraldehyde	
1-octen-3-ol	

Table 1: Koji Aroma Compounds

Another study showed that they could reproduce the aroma of koji by blending 2-methyl-2-hepten-6-one, methional, 1-octen-3-one, 1-octen-3-ol, and phenylacetaldehyde. This indicates that while phenylacetaldehyde, 1-octen-3-ol and 1-octen-3-one are the primary components of the koji aroma, a little more is needed for the full effect.

While some of these volatile compounds will not survive the brewing process they and other less obvious components will contribute to the wonderful yet subtle complexity of our saké.

Yeast – Kobo (酵母)

Yeast: a single cell fungus whose activities have been known to man for far longer than we have known about yeast itself. We have evidence of yeast being used as far back as four thousand years ago in Egypt. They used yeast for both baking and brewing. Wine was also present in this period.

In 1857 Louis Pasteur proved that fermentation was the result of living yeast rather than a chemical reaction. In this work, Pasteur showed that as oxygen is added the growth of the cell count increases and fermentation slows. Not only did this show the significance of yeast but also its two distinct modes of operation: the aerobic and the anaerobic. In the aerobic mode, yeast reproduce by budding, a process of a child cell being created and split off from the parent cell. The anaerobic mode proceeds with little to no growth in the number of cells but with increased alcohol and CO_2 production. Alcohol and CO_2 are produced in equal amounts from sugar based on the following formula:

$$C_2H_{12}O_6 \rightarrow 2C_2H_5OH + 2CO_2$$

In addition to alcohol and CO_2, over 500 other compounds are produced. These compounds contribute flavors and aromas to the ferments they produce. Some of these compounds are esters which create many of the taste and aroma differences between strains of yeast. The metabolic pathway that creates all this is pretty complex. The pamphlet, "The Fungus Among Us," gives the following pathway:[5]

---

[5] The Fungus Among Us: Yeast Culturing for HomeBrewers, Third Edition by Yuseff Cherney and Chris White, Ph.D.

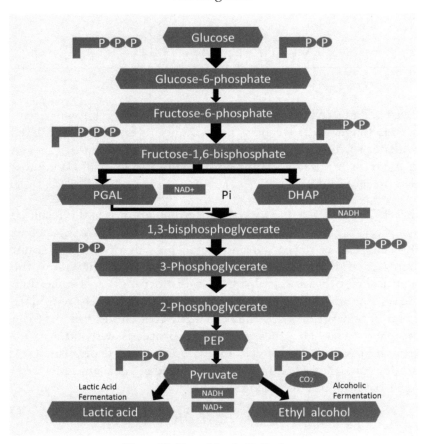

Figure 25: Yeast Metabolic Pathway

You may be thinking, "Well, this is all well and good but where does the rubber meet the saké?" It all starts with the moto. The moto is where the yeast put on some weight and buildup their cell walls to prepare for and preform a massive reproduction campaign to increase their numbers. This is the aerobic stage, where the number of yeast cells is increased to the optimal level. The open environment and frequent stirring help to supply needed oxygen for cell growth. This is the most crucial time for the yeast. Enzymes produced by the koji work on the rice to convert the rice starch into sugars for the yeast to work with. During the moto, the yeast need both the oxygen and sugar but this is not all. Yeast need other nutrients too.

Yeast need Free Amino Nitrogen (FAN). No less than 130mg/L are needed for the yeast not to struggle during fermentation; levels of 300-500mg/L are ideal. In addition to this, yeast need the following:

Chemical	mg/l
FAN	130
Ammonium Sulfate	1215
K3PO4	500
MgCl2	200
NaHSO4	50
Citric acid	2530
Sodium Citrate	2470
Bioton	0.01
Pyridoxine	0.25
Meso-inositol	1.88
Calcium Pantothenate	2.5
Thiamin	5
Peptone	25

Table 2: Needed Yeast Nutrients

Since milled rice, koji from milled rice and soft water are not the best sources for these, we (Homebrewers) often add them, or something close to them, like commercially packaged yeast nutrients.

Once the oxygen in solution starts to run out, become anaerobic, the yeast will move from reproduction to fermentation. This is not to say that reproduction will stop, it won't. However, it will slow to a trickle. The same is true for fermentation during the aerobic phase; there is a trickle. Fermentation will continue until all the sugars have been transformed into alcohol or at the point the sugar/alcohol/CO_2 mixture in the ferment overwhelms the yeasts resistance to their toxic effects.

What yeast strains are used for brewing saké? Well, back in the early 1900s the Central Brewers Union in Japan started collecting pure strains from particularly good batches of saké and made these pure strains available to all breweries. Eventually these pure strains were given numeric designations. So far there are from #1 to #16. Many breweries now use these yeast strains but there is a resurgence in the use of private strains.

In addition to these strains there are some variations that have been modified to produce less foam during fermentation. These strains, where they exist, carry the numeric designation of the parent strain numeric value times 100 plus 1. For example, strain #9's low foaming strain is #901 (#9 * 100 + 1).

For homebrew saké here in the US we have two of these strains available; #7 and #9. These strains are available from two different suppliers. Yeast #7 is available from White Labs and yeast #9 is available from Wyeast Laboratories. The details on these yeasts from their respective web sites are as follows:

Yeast	#7	#9
Description	For use in rice based fermentations. For sake, use this yeast in conjunction with koji (to produce fermentable sugar). WLP705 produces full body sake character, and subtle fragrance.	Sake #9 used in conjunction with Koji for making wide variety of Asian Jius (rice based beverages). Full bodied profile, silky and smooth on palate with low ester production.
Flocculation:	N/A	Low
Alcohol Tolerance	16%	14%
Temperature Range	>70° F (21°C)	60-75°F, 15-24°C
Attenuation	>80%	N/A
Supplier	White Labs	Wyeast Laboratories
Supplier designation	WLP705	4134

Table 3: Yeast Stains Available in the US

Yeast – Kobo (酵母)

The information these suppliers are providing is of little use to the saké homebrewer. Saké brewing generally pushes into much lower temperatures and produces alcohol levels much higher than those given on the supplier web sites. Despite this both these suppliers produce very good yeast.

As mentioned the Central Brewers Union made the pure strains they collected available to all breweries. Many breweries now use these yeast strains but many also make use of private strains.

Table 5 summarizes the Japanese saké yeasts from the Central Brewers Union. Many of these yeasts produce such high acidity that their use has fallen out of favor. These include #1 to #6, #8 and #11 to #13. This leaves less than half of those that were once in use. Of those remaining in use, saké homebrewers have easy access to only two of them; #7 and #9 as discussed previously.

As for saké yeasts that are not part of the Central Brewers Union offerings, I have not seen any structured presentation for them or how they might relate to other offerings. For example, Akita Konno carries the Brewers Union yeasts as well as others that have strain designations from Ginjo Yeast No.1 to Ginjo Yeast No. 38. So, I can't say too much more about the non-association yeasts but there are a significant number of them.

Backing up a bit, all the original yeast strains that the Central Brewers Union collected were foaming yeast strains. Over the years brewers became very familiar with these yeasts and the foam they create. So much so that they named the various stages that could be determined based on the appearance of the foam. The following table covers the foam names in order of their stage in the moromi.

Brewing Saké

Foam Stage	English Translation	Aprox. Timing
suji-awa (筋泡)	Muscle Foam	day 2-3 of Moromi
mizu-awa (水泡)	Water Foam	
iwa-awa (岩泡)	Rock Foam	
taka-awa (高泡)	High Foam	Day ~10 of Moromi
ochi-awa (落泡)	Falling Foam	
tama-awa (玉泡)	Ball Foam	
ji (地)	Land or Ground	

Table 4: Moromi Foam Names

While there were several significant events where non-foaming yeasts were unexpectedly used to brew saké it was extremely rare and considered problematic because it removed the traditional method of telling the stages of moromi.

In 1959, Mr. Takao Nihei of the Honolulu brewing company began brewing with a partially or mostly non-foaming yeast strain. He isolated the strain which had a higher percentage of non-foaming to foaming cells than are normally present. Later, a pure stain of yeast #701 was isolated from the, then, standard strain being used at the Honolulu brewing company. The way this was done was to take a fermenting mash and slowly bubble CO_2 up through the mash. The foaming strain would attach to the rising CO_2 and bubble over leaving the non-foaming yeast. After multiple prolonged fermentation sessions a virtually pure non-foaming strain exists that can be cultured to produce a pure strain.

Looking at these two strains under a microscope while in the presence of CO_2 bubbles is revealing. A CO_2 bubble with foaming yeast present literally has a shell formed by the yeast cells as they hug the surface of the bubble. CO_2 bubbles in the presence of non-foaming yeast are simply ignored by the yeast cells. What is the difference and why do non-foaming yeast cells ignore CO_2 bubbles while foaming strains don't?

Yeast – Kobo (酵母)

kyokai = Association		
Central Brewers Union Yeasts		
Kyokai #	**A.K.A.**	**Description**
#1-#6		The acidity is too strong so use has died out.
#7		Mellow fragrance, strong in fermentation. Most commonly used yeast in the country. However, used mostly for lower grade like futsushu. It once was used for ginjo but was later displaced by #9 and now #10 in this respect.
#8		The acidity is too strong so use has died out.
#9	Kumamoto Kobo	Highly flowery and fruity aromatics / fragrance, solid fermentation. Many ginjo yeasts are #9-based strains. From kura Koro.
#10	Ogawa Kobo	Low acid, fine-grained flavor, strong slow fermentation that performs best at lower temperatures. Commonly used in Tohoku. From Ibaraki prefecture brewery Meiri Shurui.
#11-#13		The acidity is too strong so use has died out.
#14	Kanazawa Kobo	Low acid, pears and apples in nose. Used a lot in Shizuoka.
#15	Akita Kobo, AK-1	Very lively fragrance and characteristic nose/flavor; but needs to ferment slowly and at low temperatures.
#16	Hachiroku - 8.6.	Super fragrant yeast from Gekkeikan Brewery.
Awa nashi kobo - The Foamless Yeasts		
#601		Same as #6 but with less foam
#701		Same as #7 but with less foam
#901		Same as #9 but with less foam
#1001		Same as #10 but with less foam
#1601		Same as #16 but with less foam
Well over 40 Non-Central Brewers Union Yeasts		

Table 5: Central Brewers Union Yeast Strains

As it turns out, foaming strains of yeast have a protein on the surface of the cell wall that is hydrophobic (eschews water) and so adhere to gas bubbles. This protein is awa1p; awa (泡) being foam and p for protein. This protein is not present on or in the cell walls of non-foaming yeast strains. Going deeper, researchers have tracked the production of the awa1p protein back to a gene (awa1) in chromosome XV. Non-foaming yeast have the gene replaced with, in at least one case for yeast #7, the left subtelomeric region of chromosome IX. Without the awa1 gene the yeast become hydrophilic (embraces water) and readily mix with water while ignoring gas bubbles.

While the presence of the awa1 gene determines whether the yeast will be foam producing or not, it has very little if any effect on all the other characteristics related to saké brewing. So in choosing between a foaming and non-foaming version of a particular yeast strain, your desire for foam is the primary if not all encompassing factor. For this reason some, old school brewers, prefer the foaming yeasts while others, looking to optimize their fermenter tank space utilization, choose the new non-foaming yeast strains.

Water – Mizu (水)

Miyamizu (宮水) – Heavenly Water – The Gold Standard?

Water is the main ingredient in all saké but it usually gets the least attention. Despite getting the least attention, water is important and plays a huge role in the quality of saké. The story that is told to demonstrate this fact is told so often that it has become like a legend.

The legend (no, the real story): Back near the end of the Edo period, 1840, Yamamura Tazaemon owned two breweries. One kura in Nishinomiya and the other in Uozaki. Tazaemon-san noticed that the saké made at Nishinomiya was always better than that made at Uozaki.

His two breweries were part of the Nada Go-go region or the five saké brewing towns of Nada. The five districts lie in a line on the coast running west to east: Mishi, Mikage and Uozaki lie in Kobe while Nishinomiya and Imazu lie in Nishinomiya. The Nada Go-go region made its fame shipping saké to Edo (Tokyo) by ship, a 20 day voyage.

Tazaemon-san struggled to figure out why the saké at Nishinomiya was always better. He ensured that they used the same rice, milled to the same level, the same conditions and equipment; nothing helped the Uozaki brewery to produce saké that was as good as that of Nishinomiya. Tazaemon-san even switched the brew masters but not even this helped. One day, Tazaemon-san, had the water used at Nishinomiya shipped to his Uozaki brewery. Saké was brewed using this water and it was as good as the saké made at Nishinomiya. Tazaemon-san had solved the mystery, it was the water!

The takeaway from this story is that good water is important if you want to make good saké. But what is "good" water for saké? Those in the Nada region would say that it is a hard water that matches the heavenly water, miyamizu. Mineral rich waters produce sakés with quick strong fermentations and are strongly flavored with full bodies. The mineral content of the miyamizu water is:

	Miyamizu (ppm)
Potassium	20
Phosphoric acid	5.2
Magnesium	5.6
Calcium	37
Chlorine	32
Sodium	32

Table 6: Miyamizu Water Makeup

This water contains the right combination of minerals that help the yeast to work vigorously. Notice that there is no iron listed. It is important that there is no iron in any water to be used for saké.

While the brewers in the Nada Go-go region had hard water to work with, much of Japan has softer water. In particular the brewers of Hiroshima had very soft water to work with. The Miura-Toji, in 1896, explained the steps needed to produce excellent saké with Hiroshima's soft water. He suggested a smaller moto be used with less koji than is normal. The koji is made at a slightly higher temperature to bring out more conversion strength. Miura's paper is "An Account of New Brewing Techniques," published in Japanese. In 1905 the Hiroshima saké, using Miura-Toji's techniques, took both first and second place in the national saké assessment. So… it seems clear that soft water, without chemical additions can also be "good" water for saké; you have to use the correct techniques though.

If soft water is used, the saké will tend to have a clean and bright but softer taste that melts in your mouth, taking with it the flavors and aromas of the saké. This is in contrast to hard water which produces a strongly flavored saké.

The recipe that most saké home brewers use has been derived from Fred Eckhardt's work[6] and is designed to work with soft water augmented with additional salts to make the water miyamizu-like.

An example of soft water is that of the Bull Run reservoir:

	Bull Run water (ppm)
Potassium	0.2
Phosphorus	0.007
Magnesium	0.9
Calcium	1.9
Chlorine	Added 2
Sodium	3.5

Table 7: Bull Run Water Makeup

You can see that the parts per million here are much lower than those of the miyamizu water. Chlorine is added to the Bull Run water to disinfect the water.

Is Miyamizu the Gold Standard? Miyamizu is clearly an excellent water for brewing saké. However, as demonstrated by the brewers of Hiroshima, their soft water can impart seductively sexy characteristics to saké that are not possible with Miyamizu.

---

[6] Beginning with "SAKE (U.S.A.)" © 1992 and followed by a series of recipe versions. His latest version being version 6.2

Brewing Salts for your water

So what do you do if you have, for example, Bull Run water which is very soft but want water like Miyamizu? Well, we can add salts to the water to increase the levels we want. This works pretty well for soft water, distilled water or reverse osmosis water but if you have hard water things are a little harder (no pun intended).

Assume we want to brew our saké with water that is equivalent to Miyamizu, the heavenly water from Nada. For this example the water we will start with is from the Bull Run Reservoir. From the tables above we can see that we need to increase the potassium from 0.2ppm to 20ppm or by 19.8ppm. That is close enough to 20ppm that we can just use 20.

Ions are usually measured in parts per million (ppm). But we need to know how many grams of potassium chloride to add. Parts per million is equivalent to milligrams per liter, mg/L, and this is just what we need.

If we want to provide the correct concentration for the moto used in the chapter "Quick Start Saké Brewing," we will need to hit 20ppm in 2.5 cups of water. 1 cup is 0.24 liters, so 2.5 cups is 0.6L.

$$0.6L * \frac{20mg}{L} = 12mg \; of \; potassium$$

Now, only 52% of potassium chloride (KCl) is potassium (see table below). So we will need:

$$\frac{12mg}{0.52} = 23mg \; of \; KCl$$

Now we can do the same for magnesium using the salt magnesium sulfate ($MgSO_4$). We want the water to have 5.6ppm of magnesium but it only has 0.9ppm. So, we need to increase magnesium by 4.5ppm.

Water – Mizu (水)

$$0.6L * \frac{4.5mg}{L} = 2.7mg \text{ of magnesium}$$

Now, again from the table, we see that only 10% of the salt is magnesium, so

$$\frac{2.7mg}{0.1} = 27mg \text{ of magnesium sulfate}$$

We could do the same for calcium and sodium. However, with each of these salts, we are adding other ions that we are not specifically interested in adding. For example, we would be adding chloride and sulfate with the above two additions. Often this is not an issue but we should not ignore them because they could reach concentrations that could have negative effects.

Common Name	Name	Chemistry	Weight g/mol	Ions	
Gypsum	Calcium Sulfate	$CaSO_4 * 2(H_2O)$	172	Ca = 23%	SO_4 = 56%
	Calcium Chloride	$CaCl_2 * 2(H_2O)$	146	Ca = 27%	Cl = 48%
	Potassium Chloride	KCl	75	K = 52%	Cl = 48%
Epsom salts	Magnesium Sulfate	$MgSO_4 * 7(H_2O)$	246	Mg = 10%	SO_4 = 39%
Chalk	Calcium Carbonate	$CaCO_3$	100	Ca = 40%	CO_3 = 60%
Table salt	Sodium Chloride	NaCL	58	Na = 40%	Cl = 60%

Table 8: Ion Makeup of Brewing Salts

So all of this will work for soft water, distilled water or water from reverse osmosis but what if you have hard water? By far the easiest thing you can do is just buy a gallon or two of distilled water from the store. Distilled water is by definition the softest water you can get. Other water from the store, like spring water, will vary but will often be just fine. You can mix this water with your tap water to dilute its hardness or use it as a base and add 100% of the ions you want.

Nihonshu-do (日本酒度) or Saké Meter Value (SMV)

Nihonshu-do also known as SMV is the way we measure the sweetness to dryness level of a saké. The word nihonshu-do itself can be broken down into three words Nihon Shu Do with the English counter parts being Japan Alcohol Degree (as in position on a scale). So Japanese Alcohol is Saké and Degree or Meter Value taken together represent the main metric used to characterize saké. At first glance this measure is relatively simple and this is as it should be for saké aficionados. A -4 SMV value for a saké implies it is quite sweet while a value of +10 would be very dry. Its use in brewing reflects its more complicated nature.

SMV was originally based on the Heavy Baume scale created by a Frenchman in the late 1700s. However, the heavy baume scale is only valid for liquids that are equal or heavier than water and this is not the case for saké. For this reason nihonshu-do has the same slope as the heavy baume scale but is not the same. When nihonshu-do and heavy baume are used to evaluate the degree of sugar in water they directly represent the amount of sugar by weight in the solution. While the baume scale is pretty much obsolete today, similar scales like the Balling, Brix and Plato scales are all attempts to measure the amount of dissolved solids in solution with more accuracy, i.e. the grams of solids in 100 grams of water. However, where Baume was working with a sodium chloride solution Balling, Brix and Plato specifically worked with sucrose solutions.

Specific Gravity, a more general concept, measures density relative to water. As dissolved solids in water raise the density when added to water it is often useful to use specific gravity. A common way to measure the SMV, degrees Baume, Balling, Brix or Plato as well as specific gravity is to use a hydrometer. A hydrometer is an instrument that floats in a solution and has values listed on its neck that are read off at the fluid level, that is where the neck breaks through the surface of the fluid. There are hydrometers encoded with all of the above systems and in some cases have more than one system covered. The denser the solution, the higher the hydrometer floats while the thinner the solution, the lower it floats.

Pure water will, by definition, have a specific gravity of 1.0 and a percent solids dissolved in solution of degrees 0.0 for SMV, Baume, Balling, Brix and Plato. For each of these, as with degrees Baume there is nowhere to go below zero (you can't have a negative amount of solids dissolved in water). However, while SMV is also 0.0 for pure water, it has values on both sides of this mark as does specific gravity. Why is this?

Well, there are a few complicating factors. The first and most prominent of these factors is alcohol. Alcohol has a specific gravity of 0.785. So when mixed with water it lowers the specific gravity of the solution. At 20% Alcohol in pure water the specific gravity is 0.957, at 15% it is 0.9678. See the following chart. The normal range for the percent of alcohol in saké is between 15% and 20%. However, 0.957 corresponds to a SMV of +65 while 0.9678 corresponds to a SMV of +48. These would be outrageously high SMV for saké, very possibly undrinkable. So how is it that saké has an SMV so much lower than these values?

As I mentioned above, dissolved solids push up the specific gravity. During and after fermentation the dissolved solids include various derivatives from starch that have not been consumed by the ferment, proteins and lipids. These push the specific gravity up to the range of roughly 0.990 (14 SMV) to 0.993 (10 SMV) for saké with 18% alcohol. In this case the contribution of the dissolved solids is 0.033, a very significant amount.

Nihonshu-do (日本酒度) or Saké Meter Value (SMV)

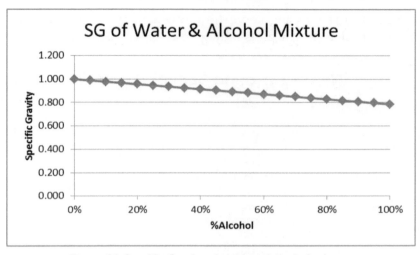

Figure 26: Specific Gravity of water and alcohol mixture

In order to get a better feel for how these metrics relate to each other I have plotted each against the SMV (Nihonshu-do value on x-axis). Recall that neither Baume nor Plato is valid below zero though this is not indicated on the chart.

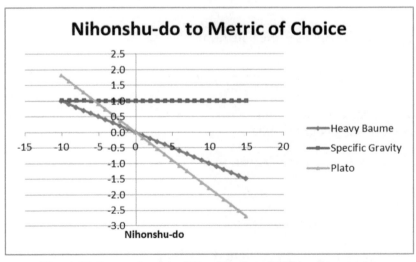

Figure 27: Conversion from Nihonshu-do or SMV to other metrics

75

To get a better feeling about how specific gravity changes with SMV, the chart below plots only specific gravity against SMV.

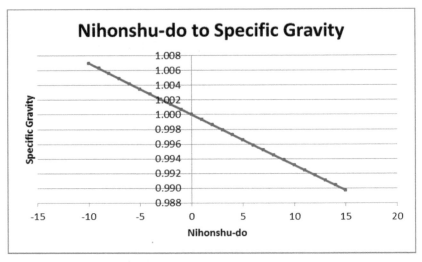

Figure 28: Conversion from SMV to SG

The formulas and table used for graphing these two charts are as follows:

Specific Gravity uses the equation:

$$S.G. = \frac{m}{m + SMV} \text{ where } m \text{ is } 1443$$

There are several m values that exist for Baume but this is the correct one taken for SMV.

Heavy Baume uses the equation:

$$H.B. = -SMV/10$$

Plato uses the equation:

$$Plato = 260 * \left(1 - \frac{(m + SMV)}{m}\right) \text{ where } m \text{ is } 1443$$

Nihonshu-do (日本酒度) or Saké Meter Value (SMV)

Nihonshu-do	Heavy Baume	Specific Gravity	Plato
-10	1.0	1.007	1.80
-9	0.9	1.006	1.62
-8	0.8	1.006	1.44
-7	0.7	1.005	1.26
-6	0.6	1.004	1.08
-5	0.5	1.003	0.90
-4	0.4	1.003	0.72
-3	0.3	1.002	0.54
-2	0.2	1.001	0.36
-1	0.1	1.001	0.18
0	0.0	1.000	0.00
1	-0.1	0.999	-0.18
2	-0.2	0.999	-0.36
3	-0.3	0.998	-0.54
4	-0.4	0.997	-0.72
5	-0.5	0.997	-0.90
6	-0.6	0.996	-1.08
7	-0.7	0.995	-1.26
8	-0.8	0.994	-1.44
9	-0.9	0.994	-1.62
10	-1.0	0.993	-1.80
11	-1.1	0.992	-1.98
12	-1.2	0.992	-2.16
13	-1.3	0.991	-2.34
14	-1.4	0.990	-2.52
15	-1.5	0.990	-2.70

Table 9: Conversion values between SMV, HB, SG and Plato

The lighter gray sections of the table represent invalid entries created by extending the slope of the line.

Another important wrinkle to all of this is that temperature matters. What does this mean? Well, because water, alcohol and other liquids vary in their volume with temperature their density also varies. This means that all of these metrics will vary with the temperature of the solution. For the information above, 60°F is assumed. However, as the various solutions are mixtures of their constituent components, each expanding at their own rates making all but gross adjustments for temperature impractical.

To adjust degrees Plato, add or subtract 0.0278 for each degree above or below 60°F. To adjust the specific gravity, add or subtract 0.00011 for each degree above or below 60°F.

The thing to keep in mind while using these systems is that SMV measures relative dryness, Plato measures the percentage of solids (percent sugar of solution with no alcohol) and specific gravity measures the relative weight compared to water (i.e., times the weight of water in the same volume).

Also, there is another way to make these measurements, with a refractometer. This is covered in the chapter "Measuring your Saké."

Sando (酸度) – Acidity

The acidity of a saké or its sando is a measure of how much acid in grams per liter is present in the saké. Acidity in saké balances its sweetness. The sweeter the saké the higher its acidity can be without being sour or annoying. In general the higher acidity the thinner the saké will seem. However, as with all the characteristic parameters of saké, we cannot say that a saké with a high acidity level will seem thin, only thinner than if it had lower acidity.

Acidity levels tend to range from 0.8 to 1.7. As we saw previously, the nihonshu-do values (SMV) tend to be between -5 and +10. Using these two metrics together is more useful than individually. Recall that the more negative the nihonshu-do value the sweeter it is and the more positive the dryer it is. So producing a saké with SMV -4 and acidity of 1.7 (two extremes) could create a heavy dry saké; that's right, dry. This is because the acidity balances out all of the sweetness. We must keep in mind that these are only trends and not absolutes. In the same way, if we produce a saké with high SMV of +7 and an acidity of 0.8, it may be sweet and thin or watery.

The acidity comes naturally from several contributors: oenococcus, pediococcus and lactobacillus bacteria (lactic acid), acetic acid bacteria including acetobacters (acetic acid) and yeast (succinic acid, malic acid, citric acid, D-lactic acid, inosinic acid). However, the most common method for producing the moto is sokujo moto where the majority of the non-yeast produced lactic acid (L-lactic acid) is added directly rather than through bacteria cultivation as is done for kimoto and yamahai moto. D-lactic acid produced by yeast during fermentation generally falls in the range of 140mg/L to 270mg/L. L-lactic acid levels are more easily controlled by the brewer, generally fall in a broader range of 60mg/L to 450mg/L.

These acids provide a flavor component as well as their balancing effects. Lactic acid has a smooth acidity but can approach astringency. Acetic acid is the acid in vinegar. Succinic acid adds a slight heaviness and earthiness; a common taste that is a combination of saltiness, bitterness and acidity. Malic acid is light with some bitterness. Finally, citric acid brings a strong astringency. The relative ratio of these acids as well as amino acids (not discussed here) offer dials for the brewer to adjust.

A major goal for saké brewers is to strike a good balance in the acid levels with each other, with the sweet / dry level and other components so they come together for a nicely unified experience. Kimoto and yamahai moto procedures are largely about balancing these acid levels while sokujo moto is more direct – measure and add.

Amino Sando (アミノ酸度) – Amino Acid

As with acidity, the amino acid level of a saké or its amino sando levels are a measure of how much amino acid is in the saké. Amino sando along with the sugar levels largely determine the viscosity and chewiness of a saké.

Amino sando levels tend to vary between about 0.7 and 1.4. The lower the amino sando value the thinner the saké tends to be; this opens up the saké. Higher levels of amino sando are accompanied by higher viscosity and rounder flavors.

Umami, an important flavor component is tied to the amino acid glutamate. As amino sando rises and falls, glutamate also tends to rise and fall, so reaching an ideal umami level is achieved by adjusting the amino sando levels. Researchers from Akita Prefectural University found that of the 20 or more amino acids in saké four are most important.[7]

They found four amino acids[8] that are strongly related to saké taste components and that the total concentrations are less important for taste than is the balance of these four. They demonstrated that through the manipulation of the choice of rice, milling levels, koji production and both yeast aerobic and anaerobic processes the balance could be controlled to create high quality saké.

---

[7] Search for amino acids affecting the taste of sake by Iwano Kimio et. al., from the Akita Prefectural University in Journal of the Brewing Society of Japan 2004, Volume 99, No. 9, Pages 659-664.
[8] The four amino acids are: alanine, arginine, glutamic acid, and aspartic acid.

Amino Acid	Taste Component
Alanine	Sweetness
Arginine	Bitterness
Glutamic Acid	Complex: acidity, astringency and other flavor components
Aspartic Acid	Complex: acidity, astringency and other flavor components

Table 10: Four Primary Amino Acids for Taste

A side note related to amino acids: The reason the existence of iron in water to be used for saké is such a problem is that the iron attaches to the center of a compound attached to an amino acid from koji. In this position it darkens the saké and changes the taste and aroma for the worse. In addition, iron speeds up a reaction between residual sugars and amino acids that change the taste and aroma of the saké over time.

Protecting your Homebrew Saké from light

Saké, as with beer, is sensitive to light and in particular ultraviolet light. Sunlight is the greatest offender having a much higher degree of ultraviolet light than most other sources. This is not to say that other sources like florescent lights are harmless, they can have a negative impact as well. Given that saké can be harmed by this light and light is all around us, what can we do to keep our saké safe from this harm?

We can choose to use bottles that have the best properties for filtering the light and specifically the ultraviolet light. Fortunately for us, Bradley E. Sturgeon, PhD[9] recently did a study that examined which colors of glass bottles provide the best light filtering.

Visible light runs from about 400nm to 700nm in wave length with the shorter wave lengths being of higher energy. Ultraviolet light is in the range of about 280nm to 380nm, just below that of visible light. These high energy waves damage saké by damaging the amino acids and vitamins in saké causing it to turn yellowish or more yellowish and develop an off putting aroma.

Based on Bradley's data displayed in the following chart which covers most of the ultraviolet range, blue glass stops (absorbs) only a little more than 70% at 325nm and then drops down to less than 20% for 350nm and 400nm. Green glass does a little better but neither blue nor green come close to the effectiveness of brown glass. Brown glass stops 96% or better over this range.

---

[9] Bradley E. Sturgeon Supplemental paper to Basic Brewing Episode Airing April 10th 2008
http://c2.libsyn.com/media/18257/bbrskunking.pdf?nvb=20101023235544&nva=20101025000544&sid=5da75927c6aef854fce3161a006d9cf6&l_sid=18257&l_eid=&l_mid=1511404&t=080c8274ab3556625c6ff

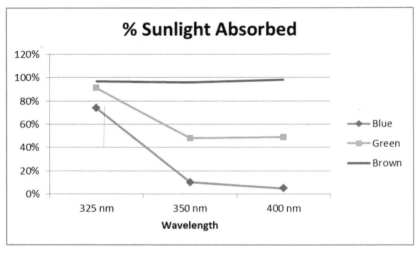

Figure 29: Percent of Light Absorbed and Unable to Harm Saké Contents

A second way to look at this data is to look at the intensity of the light that gets through the filter (is not absorbed). The chart below shows this data along with the intensity of the light from the sun unfiltered. The blue bottle has very little effect. Green does a little better. But brown stops most of the light at these wave lengths. In fact, brown seems to do the best for all light sources up to about 500nm.

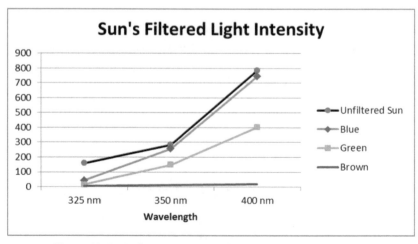

Figure 30: Light Intensity Shining Through Bottle to Contents

Sanitation

Saké Brewing: Cleanliness is next to godliness

For making saké, as with other fermented beverages, cleanliness and sanitation are extremely important. The reason for this is that a goodly part of the flavors come from the "bugs" (bacteria and yeast) in the ferment. When the bugs are the ones we want, we get the flavors we desire. But when others invade the party, they produce off flavors that lower the quality or even ruin the beverage altogether.

In saké using the sokujo-moto method there is one player (bug) that we want to encourage while restraining all others. The player we want is the yeast we introduce ourselves. When using the yamahai-moto method there are two main players; lactobacilli and yeast.

Given this, how do we go about restraining all the other bugs? Well, restraining these other bugs is a key part of saké brewing. It begins before we even start to prepare the ingredients; it starts with the cleaning of the equipment. Once clean, we sanitize the equipment as needed throughout the process. We control the pH and temperature to provide an environment discomforting for most bugs and finally, when not making namazake or unpasteurized saké, we pasteurize the saké at least once, usually twice.

Here I want to cover the basics of sanitation needed for making saké. To sanitize something, it must first be clean. If not, bacteria (bugs) have places to hide preventing us from satisfactorily sanitizing. What does it mean to be clean? It means that all the foreign matter has been removed and none remains. However, this does not include bacteria and other microorganisms that may be present. Once clean an object can be sanitized. Sanitization kills off many of these bugs so that they remain only at negligible levels.

Removing, killing and simply destroying 100% of these critters is called sterilization.

For most elements of making saké we only need to worry about cleaning and sanitizing. Sterilization is important for yeast management but once we have the needed yeast in hand we are good to go; no more sterilization required.

OK, so what do we need to know to clean our equipment? Well, cleaning is all about applying the effort needed to remove all the foreign matter, the places where bugs hide. To lower the effort required to do this we can use chemicals; detergent, bleach or something called percarbonates are the most commonly used.

It is important to avoid cleaning detergents and agents with perfumes. These can be absorbed into plastic and later your brew. It is also important to rinse thoroughly to remove the lingering film common to detergents. Any remaining film can negatively affect the taste of your saké.

Bleach can be mixed with cold water to produce a caustic agent (high pH) that will dissolve organic deposits; 1 tablespoon per gallon works well. However, you must be careful when using with metals because its corrosive powers will pit metals if left in contact for too long. Brass and copper are the extreme cases here and should not be cleaned using bleach.

Percarbonates make up a group of cleaners that are specialized for the food industry and commonly found in use by brewers. The one that comes to my mind is, PBW, Powder Brewery Wash. This product is very effective while rinsing away easily. Use 1 tablespoon per gallon.

Use any of these cleaners or none of them but be sure your equipment is clean. Once you have done this, and you are just about ready to use your equipment it is time to sanitize it. Both chemicals and heat can be used to sanitize. Bleach, Iodophor and a product called Star San are all good chemical choices.

Sanitation

Bleach mixed with water at a ratio of 1 tablespoon bleach to 1 gallon of water provides the needed killing power to sanitize an object left to soak for 20 minutes. Technically speaking, you don't need to rinse the object after draining but many will rinse with boiled water.

Iodophor mixed with water provides a very nice sanitizer. No more than 1 tablespoon per 5 gallons of water is required and it is no more effective at higher concentrations. Whereas you need to soak objects in bleach for a considerable time, only 2 minutes are needed to soak them in iodophor. Also, you do not need to rinse after soaking in iodophor. There is one drawback however, after prolonged exposure, iodophor will stain plastics. The "damage" is only cosmetic and does not affect the suitability of your equipment.

Star San, an even faster acting sanitizer, is made specifically for brewing by the same people who make PBW. This product will sanitize your item in 30 seconds and like those above, does not need to be rinsed away.

While plastic items are not as amenable to heat sanitation, glass and metal items are. For example using your dishwasher is a good way to sanitize bottles en mass. As discussed, all items must already be clean. While doing this it is best not to use any detergents, just let the dishwasher go through its cycle and the heat and steam will do the sanitization.

While there can be a lot more said about heat for sanitization and even sterilization the only other use most may do is a form of "flaming" an item. This is a quick way to sterilize it before use. I use this for quickly sanitizing my stirring spoon.

This basic information is everything you need to know for your saké brewing. While all your equipment should be clean, only those items that come in contact with the saké as it progresses through the brewing process need to be sanitized.

Seimai (精米) or Rice Milling / Polishing

The level of polishing or milling of the rice has a major impact on the characteristics of the saké we produce. The characteristic difference is a function of the amounts of proteins, fats and oils that remain in the rice used for brewing. The more of these that can be removed the more refined the saké. This is why daiginjo has a higher milling rate (i.e., lower seimaibuai) than ginjo. Since the proteins, fats and oils have the highest concentrations on the outer portions of rice with steadily dropping concentrations the further from the outer edge you get, going from 90% seimaibuai to 85% has a greater impact than going from 60% to 55% seimaibuai.

The methods used to mill our rice determines how effective the milling is at removing proteins, fats, and oils without wasting starch. Imagine that the level of concentration declines linearly with distance from the surface. Then removing a square unit of the outer 1% will remove more proteins, fats and oils than removing a square unit of the second 1% (from 1% down to 2%). Based on this we would want to mill our rice, such that, we uniformly remove the outer most layers down to the desired seimaibuai. The method to do this is called the Flat Rice Polishing method.

While the Flat Rice Polishing method is good, Daishichi has developed a method that is a step better. It is called the Super-Flat Rice Polishing method and works better because it focuses on the amount of high concentration material it removes. To better understand this let's back up and consider four different ways of, or goals for, milling rice. These are:

- The conventional method
- The grain shaped method
- The flat rice method
- The super-flat rice method

The first of these is the conventional method and is used for almost all rice milling today. It is optimized to mill the rice as quickly as possible while keeping rice cracking to a minimum.

Modern saké rice polishing proceeds by circulating rice being milled passed a milling stone. The milling stone spins around a vertical axis with the rice dropped through a chamber around the outer edge of the milling stone where it may contact the stone and have some small part removed. The rice is then circulated back up above the stone where it will again be dropped. This pattern of circulation past the milling stone can continue for days depending on the amount of material to be removed.

The conventional method proceeds with the milling stone turning at a very fast rate and controlling the amount of rice in the milling chamber to allow for considerable free motion for each grain of rice. This results in the rice having a tendency to fall through the chamber with its long axis being horizontal and hence the most likely parts to come in contact with the milling stone are the edges and the ends which results in a rounder milled grain. The following illustration shows how the milled rice changes in shape as milling proceeds. The outer darker gray represents the original size of the rice before milling while the inner lighter gray shape represents the evolving shape of the milled rice as more and more of the rice is milled away. In each of the three milling stages shown, both a front and side view of the grain is given to help you imagine the full three dimensional shape.

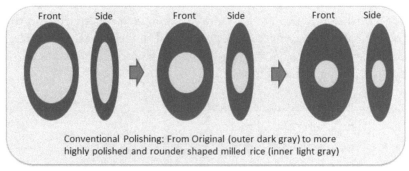

Figure 31: Conventional Polishing Method Results

Seimai (精米) or Rice Milling / Polishing

As can be seen in this illustration, the distance from the top of the original grain to the top of the milled grain is changing much more than the distance from the side of the original grain to the side of the milled grain. Another way of saying this is that the percentage of milling along the long axis of the grain is higher than the percentage of the milling along the width or depth axis.

Second is the grain shaped milling method. With this method the goal is to reduce the grain by the same percentage on each axis. While considered to be the ideal method for some time, it still has a tendency to remove too much material from the longer axis. Say the long axis was twice as long as the depth axis, then removing the same percentage from the long and depth axis would mean that we are removing twice as much material from the long axis than from the depth axis. While this method is more balanced than the standard method it does not do as well as the flat rice method we mentioned above.

Third is the flat rice method that we discussed above. In this method a smaller amount, percentagewise, is milled from the longer axes than from the shortest axis. However the milling distance from the original rice surface is equal for every axis. The following illustration shows how the material that is milled away remains the same thickness all the way around the milled rice that remains; that is the dark gray ring around the milled rice is the same width no matter where you measure it.

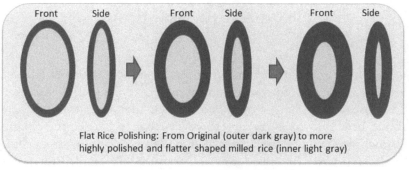

Flat Rice Polishing: From Original (outer dark gray) to more highly polished and flatter shaped milled rice (inner light gray)

Figure 32: Flat Rice Polishing Results

Finally, the fourth method is the super-flat rice milling method developed by Daishichi Saké Brewery. In this method the goal is to remove more material from the flat part of the rice than the edges or the ends. Doing this removes more of the unwanted material and leaves the milled rice flatter and longer proportionally than the flat rice method.

For the most part the way we get from the conventional method to the super-flat rice method is by slowing down the speed at which the milling stone spins around the vertical axis and increasing the amount of rice falling through the milling chamber at any point in time. The added rice in the chamber causes more of the rice to fall with the long axis in a vertical position. This prevents the ends from striking the mill stone more frequently than the other surfaces.

Daishichi has found that using their super-flat rice polishing method to polish rice to a seimaibuai of 70% removes the same amount of unwanted materials (proteins, fats, oils, ash and minerals) as milling rice using the conventional method to a seimaibuai of 58%. So using the super-flat method saves 12% of the rice material while removing an equal amount of undesirable material. One drawback of using this super-flat rice polishing method is that it takes longer. It can take three times as long to get down to the same seimaibuai or twice as long to get down to the equivalent level of unwanted material being removed.

Homebrew Solution

While these methods are the first step used for commercial saké brewing they are currently out of reach of homebrewers. For homebrewers, milling is not much more than the story we hear about how the pros do it. However, this is hardly acceptable. Homebrewers have, to my knowledge, only two options for milling levels; standard white rice (approximately 90-93%) and Ginjo grade

Seimai (精米) or Rice Milling / Polishing

rice (60%). For those who would like to brew other classes of saké more options are needed.

Looking into rice milling methods we find that there are a number of personal rice polishers on the market that can be used. These personal machines are, of course, not meant for milling rice for saké but rather for table rice. The TwinBird Mill is one such machine.

For saké brewing, we want to be able to mill rice anywhere from table rice levels (about 90%) to daiginjo levels (less than or equal to 50%). Maybe even lower levels. Could the TwinBird do the trick? The short answer is yes, but...

The TwinBird (www.twinbird.com) MR-D570 will mill up to about 4 go at a time. Hmmm, 4 go, well a go is 180ml volume. 1 go of Hitomebore white rice I measured weighs 161 grams. This weight will vary depending on the grain size and moisture. Anyway, 10 pounds is ~4540 grams or ~28 go, which is about what is needed for a "standard" small batch of saké.

Let's look at two cases for milling rates that we may want to do. This first is to mill to just less than 70%. This is the milling rate that used to be required for both Junmai and Honjozo saké. While the legal milling rate restrictions for the Junmai classification have been removed most of the Junmai saké produced still follow this guideline. The second case is to mill the rice to just less than 50%. This milling level will give us a Daiginjo or Junmai Daiginjo classification.

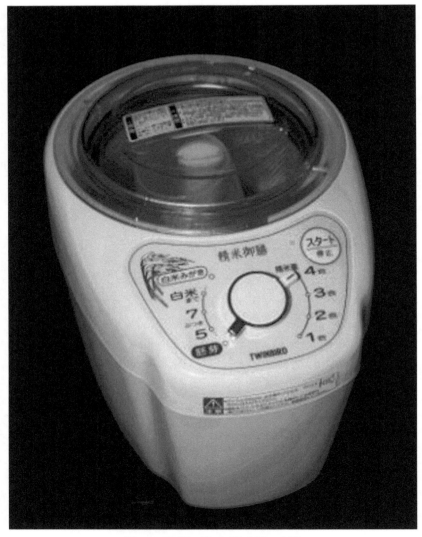

Figure 33: The TwinBird Rice Mill

Case 1: Again using the Hitomebore as a concrete example, we want to know how much rice we need to purchase and mill. If we buy brown Hitomebore we simply divide the amount we need in the recipe by the milling rate we want:

Seimai (精米) or Rice Milling / Polishing

$$14.3 lbs = \frac{10 lbs}{0.7} \text{ or in go}: 40.2 = \frac{28.2 go}{0.7}$$

However, it is more likely that we will want to buy Hitomebore that has already been milled to a white rice level. White rice is generally milled to somewhere between 90% and 93%. Making this adjustment gives:

$$13.3 lbs = 14.3 lbs * 0.93 \text{ or in go } 37.4 go = 40.2 go * 0.93$$

Case 2: Still using Hitomebore and the same process as in case 1, we can straight away calculate the amount of white rice we need to purchase as:

$$18.6 lbs \text{ white rice} = \frac{10 lbs \text{ milled rice}}{0.5 \text{ milling rate}} * 0.93 \text{ white rice rate}$$

This same calculation gives 52.4 go.

Why do I keep calculating the amount in go? Because the TwinBird mill's batch size is measured in go and I want to be able to know how many batches I will need to mill. Since the largest batch size for the TwinBird is 4 go, case 1 will have 9.4 batches and case 2 will have 13.1 batches. For this discussion we will assume that each batch remains as a single quantity that does not mix with other batches. This clearly leaves open the possibility of more efficient methods but it will simplify our thinking and discussion.

There are a few more items we will need to consider while milling. First the goal is to mill the rice to the desired level while not breaking or cracking the rice. Broken grains expose the core / heart directly and may retain more of the outer layers than we would like. Cracked grains can also expose the heart or make it too easy for steam and koji mold to enter. If the steam gets into the heart it will produce overly mushy rice that is not good for growing high quality koji. To produce the best quality enzymes, koji needs to be able to get into the rice and grow. But if it is too easy to get down into the rice or the rice is too mushy, the best quality enzymes will not be produced.

Commercial brewers will slow the milling process down as much as they can with their equipment to more gently strip away the outer layers. This also limits the amount of heating and cooling that can contribute to rice cracking. As the rice heats up and its inner layers are exposed during the milling process it loses much of its moisture. This makes it even more brittle and vulnerable to cracking and breaking. While milling our own rice we need to be aware of these processes and avoid them and their negative consequences.

What characteristics does the TwinBird mill have in these respects? How much of the outer layer does it take off over how much time? How much does it heat the rice? Can I adjust these? Well, it depends, ~10°F, not so much. Let's look a little closer.

I did a limited experiment where I use 4 go of the Hitomebore rice in the TwinBird mill with the mill set to run for 4 go with brown rice. Setting it for brown rice makes it run its maximum time before automatically stopping. With this setting the mill runs for somewhere between 5 and 6 minutes. Running the mill repeatedly I captured the following data:

Mill Activations	Seimai Buai	Grams
-1	100	694
0	93	645
1	86	597
2	82	569
3	79	546
4	75	523
5	72	501
6	69	477

Table 11: TwinBird Milling Data

The -1 activation represents brown rice that has not been milled. It was calculated based on a 93% seimaibuai for white rice. Seimaibuai

Seimai (精米) or Rice Milling / Polishing

is the percentage rice left over after milling. The 0th activation is thus the data for white rice, the real starting point. Each of the following activation data represents the rice after that number of times in the mill as it runs for its 5 to 6 minutes. One key point is that the more rice (by weight) the more effective and faster the milling process. In this discussion we will not make use of this fact but in the design of more efficient and less time consuming methods it would be important. This data is given in the chart below:

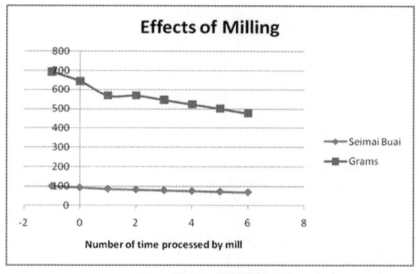

Figure 34: Rice Milling Data

As the initial batch is milled its seimaibuai drops by 7, 4 and 3, 3, 3, 3 finally reaching 69% after 6 activations. If run continuously, this batch could be mill to 69% in about 36 minutes. This means that we could mill all 9.4 batches needed in 6 hours nonstop. However, things are rarely so simple. Recall that each run is heating the rice by about 10°F. The mill basket is also heating up significantly which implies the rice will heat more each run than the last.

Leaving the rice to cool in a bowl will work but is slow (slow may be better with less cracking but I did not look at this). It would be faster to spread it out over a cookie sheet or the like. The following chart is based on a single batch cooling in a bowl over time.

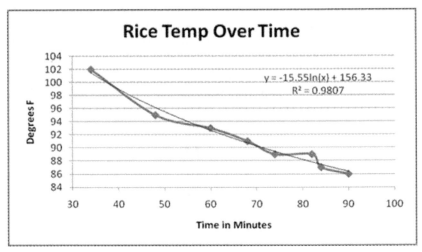

Figure 35: Rice Cooling Time

Interleaving batches may be a good way to go to ensure the rice does not take on too much heat. This would give each batch about 40 minutes to lose the approximate 10°F it gained in the mill. While more complex than exclusively concentrating on a single batch until it is done, this would still be able to get you close to the 6 hours time but without risking heat related damage. Now that we have a time period that the milling could, theoretically, be finished, we need to acknowledge that the milling machine was NEVER meant to operate on a continuous basis like this. Nor have I explored the limits of the machine as I did the above 6 activations over a period of 2 hours.

After the rice has been milled to the desired level it needs to rest to move back to an ambient temperature and to absorb enough moisture so that when washed and soaked it will not crack from taking on moisture too rapidly. A day exposed to the moisture in the air may do the trick but it might take even longer.

Seimai (精米) or Rice Milling / Polishing

Finally, in other experiments I was able to get some rice down under 20% and even below 10%. What I cannot tell though is how much of these grains, so highly polished, are truly from the center of the rice. At these levels I notice that the nuka (rice flour or shavings) is getting pretty coarse. I did not see this with larger grains.

I conclude from this that it is possible for those who really want to, to use this mill for their saké brewing. Practically speaking, it may take many sessions over several days to mill your own rice for a batch of saké. However, for those with less time this mill is not a practical solution. The TwinBird and other personal milling machines, show a way that slightly larger milling machines can be built for homebrewers to have more flexibility in milling levels.

Rice Preparation

Preparing Your Rice for Saké Brewing

An important step performed several times during the saké brewing process is the preparation of the rice. We prepare rice for the moto, then again for each step of the san-dan-jikomi, the three step addition of rice, koji and water to build up to the moromi or the main fermentation. The preparation of the rice is the same for each of these additions.

Rice preparation consists of washing, rinsing, soaking, draining, packing, steaming, cooling and finally adding it to the brew. Rice for koji also goes through the same process except rather than adding it to the brew it is inoculated and then incubated.

White rice, whether milled as table rice or milled to a higher degree specifically for brewing saké, has unwanted material on it that we need to remove. This material can simply be the rice flour from the milling process. However, sometimes other material is added to assist with milling, e.g. talc and other material is added to enhance or enrich the final product. The later often include several of the following: Folic Acid, Niacin, Iron, Zinc, Selenium and Vitamins B-1, B-12 and E. Washing the rice in cold water removes these particulates. This can remove iron that contributes to bad taste development in saké and surface powders that can cause the steamed rice to be stickier than we would like.

Once thoroughly washed the rice should be rinsed in cold running water to rinse away the particulates that have been washed free. In some cases you may choose to do both the wash and rinse in a single step with cold running water. You know you are done when the water that starts with milky white run off turns clear.

Now that we have clean milled rice we want to raise its water content up to 25 to 35%. Commercial brewers are very specific about how much water they want the rice to absorb. In fact they have different amounts for their various styles and whether the rice will be used for making koji or not. In some cases, brewers use a stop watch to make sure the rice does not soak for too long and take up too much water. Anyway, soaking the rice in cold water is the method used. The time needed to reach the desired water uptake level depends on the temperature of the water as well as the type and milling rate (seimaibuai) of the rice.

If the rice is to be used for making koji and the uptake of water is too little the rice will not steam properly leaving a hard uncooked center that the koji mold will not penetrate. On the other hand having too much water uptake will cause the rice to be too mushy and sticky after steaming. This mushy rice base is too easy for the koji mold to penetrate and in turn prevents or lowers production of the transformative enzymes we want. Most rice used for homebrew saké will need to steep between 30 minutes and two hours. As homebrewers we are more often than not more guilty of soaking too much than too little.

We don't need to be as particular as commercial brewers about the amount of uptake but rather shoot for the general ball park. To hit this ball park using rice with a 60% seimaibuai, soak the rice in cold water for one hour. If you are using rice milled as table rice, seimaibuai 90 to 93%, soak for two hours. While these times are close to best, the additional water uptake from a much longer soaking period has only a small impact on the saké as long as it is not used to make koji. For this reason, some brewers soak their rice over night to get an early start on steaming in the morning.

As you get better at brewing saké you may want to be more exacting in the water uptake level. To do this, you can add an experiment for the particular type of rice you use. Wash and rinse some rice and divide it into 5 equal portions. Weigh and record the results. Place all portions into cold water to soak. At 30 minute increments remove one portion, thoroughly drain and weigh. The percentage water uptake is the final weight divided by the starting weight minus 1 with the result multiplied by 100. Plotting these five points against their soak time will give you a curve you can use to determine how long you should soak your rice for the uptake you desire.

$$Water\ uptake\ \% = \left(\frac{Final\ weight}{Starting\ weight} - 1\right) * 100$$

Getting back to the topic at hand, once the rice has soaked for the period we want, it is time to start draining the rice. Leaving the rice sit in a colander, strainer or sieve for about an hour will do the trick. Once nicely drained, it is time to prepare for steaming the rice.

To steam the rice we want to ensure the steam has to rise up through our rice to get out of the pot. We control this with the proper packing of our drained rice into our steamer. We want to have an even layer of rice that covers the entire steamer base (or each level of the steamer we will use). Ensure the rice evenly covers the base out all the way to the walls of the steamer so no steam can find a quick path to escape without going through the rice bed. Laying down a layer of cheese cloth or butter muslin before packing the rice will ease cleanup. With the rice packed into the steamer we are ready to steam.

Having drained the rice, we steam the rice for somewhere between 45 minutes and one hour. To tell when the rice has been steaming for long enough, examine a rice kernel, cut it in half, it should be uniformly gelatinized. If you bite into it, it should have a consistent resistance all the way through; firm but not hard. In general, steam the rice for 45 minutes. Be sure to check the water level in your steamer about half way through to make sure you have enough water. Running dry can destroy your steamer; smoke your rice or both.

With the rice steamed, lay it out on something like a cookie sheet where it can cool and dry. While it is cooling break all the clumps apart so that all the individual grains are as separate as possible. The washing and rinsing steps help here; by removing the outer starchy coating on the rice there is less sticky surface after steaming. By the time you have the rice clumps all broken apart, the rice should be mostly cool or at least cool enough to move to the final step before use. If the rice is to be added to the brew as steamed rice, it should be cooled further. Use of a little cold water, as in the Quick Start Brewing Method is OK. On the other hand, if the rice is to be used for making koji, it can be inoculated with koji-kin.

So there you have it, rice preparation for saké brewing, hhhoo-yah!

Koji Making

What are we trying to do while making koji?

OK, so what exactly are we trying to do when making koji? Well, to examine this we need to consider the role koji plays in Saké Brewing. In saké brewing we use koji to provide a wide variety of products. These include products that provide flavor and aroma elements as well as enzymes which degrade proteins and starches into smaller component parts. For example proteins are disassembled into peptides and amino acids while starches are converted into smaller starches, dextrins and sugars.

Rice starts out with 7% to 8% protein, but the higher polished the rice the less protein will be left. However, even with lower levels of milling we do not focus on koji's production of enzymes to break down this protein. Rice starch is our main focus and needs to be broken down as effectively as possible into sugars. Koji produces alpha, beta and gamma amylase. Depending on how we culture the koji, we can emphasize protein or starch degrading enzymes. High temperature cultivation, 98°F to 104°F, leads to the production of saccharification enzymes whereas lower temperature cultivation, from 98°F down to 68°F, emphasizes protein degrading enzymes. So to make good koji for saké brewing we must culture the koji at the higher temperature range.

Another important aspect of cultivation is to ensure that koji mycelia reach deep into the grain. When the mycelia work hard to bore into the grain more saccharification enzymes are produced. The primary factor that can prevent the mycelia from boring into the grain is when the grain is too moist and the fungi can get all the moisture it needs from the surface. Under these conditions the fungi will produce a small amount of enzymes which will go to work right away in the moist environment on the surface to produce sugar. With the readily available sugar for the fungus there is no need for it to push into the grain or produce more enzymes. Koji produced under these conditions and with these results is called Nurihaze koji. Nurihaze koji is generally not desirable.

Tsukihaze koji or koji with the mycelia reaching deep into the grain but only sparsely covering the surface is produced using ½ the koji-kin with rice that has about 38% moisture[10] after steaming and has been cooled such that the surface of each grain is relatively dry. Too dry and the koji-kin (spores) will not stick properly but beyond that it should be dry. Then, cultivating with moist air for the first day enables the koji to get a good start. The lower the seimaibuai, milling rate of the rice, the less humid the air should be. For example, a brown rice would be safer in a more humid environment. On the second day, moving to dryer conditions helps the koji mycelia to move into the grain. Tsukihaze koji is used primarily for ginjo and daiginjo style sakés.

A koji that is between Nurihaze and Tsukihaze koji is Sohaze koji which is the most common koji used for saké brewing. In Sohaze koji the entire surface of the grain is fully covered but the mycelia does not always penetrate as far into the grain as it does with Tsukihaze. For this reason, Sohaze koji at the lower end of the saccharification power range is used in circumstances where there is less need to produce sugars; for example, the moto. However, Sohaze at the higher end of the saccharification power is fully capable of converting all the starch that is possible to convert. Sohaze koji with low saccharification power has mycelia that do not reach far into the grain while sohaze koji with a high saccharification power has mycelia that reaches deep into the grain, much like Tsukihaze koji does.

The main difference between making tsukihaze and sohaze styles is that only half the koji-kin is used in making tsukihaze.

---

[10] As seen in the last chapter, moisture uptake can be measured with the change in weight. Absolute moisture content can be measured in the same way by starting with moist rice and driving off the moisture.

Of the three amylase enzymes produced alpha and gamma are the most prevalent but because of the low pH of the mash alpha amylase has a very low activity level. Alpha amylase is well suited for a pH of 5.5 but a saké mash will be closer to a pH of 3. Gama amylase on the other hand thrives at a pH of 3 and produces glucose. The very low temperature of the mash inhibits all of the enzymes which slows the rate of sugar production to a trickle. The slow rate of sugar being added to the mash helps the yeast stay healthy longer than in fermentation where there is a high concentration of sugar at the start. A high concentration of sugar increases the osmotic stress on the yeast cell walls. This increased osmotic pressure causes the yeast to shut down sooner than they might with lower levels. It is this characteristic of the saké brewing process that allows saké to reach the high alcohol levels it does.

In order to make koji for brewing saké we need to prepare the rice as discussed in the last chapter. After following all the steps listed there, and you have the clumps of rice broken apart, it is time to prepare the koji starter. Koji starter, koji-kin, Aspergillus oryzae, all names for the same thing, is usually provided as a powder containing the spores that will inoculate the newly steamed rice. Only a small amount of this powder is needed. Because of the relatively small amount of powder, it can be difficult to spread it evenly over all the rice.

A trick I learned from the people at Gem Cultures is to take a small amount of flour and toast it in a dry pan until it is lightly toasted. After the toasted flour has cooled, we can then mix it with the koji-kin to double the amount of powder. This makes it much easier to evenly distribute the powder over the rice for a uniform inoculation. The toasting is, in effect, sanitizing the flour to make it safe for use. Without toasting there is a danger that bugs present in the flour could get a foot hold in the koji and cause the batch to go bad. Whether you add the flour or not is up to you since it is just to make it easier.

While the rice is still warm but less than 115°F, maybe around 100°F is good, sprinkle some of the koji-kin over the rice; about

1/3rd of the total powder. Mix the rice and koji-kin well and spread out again. Repeat by sprinkling the next 1/3rd of the powder and mixing well until all the koji-kin has been mixed very well with the rice. As much as possible we want to cover every grain of rice with a bit of koji-kin. Wrap the mixture in a tightly woven cloth that will breathe but not stick to the rice. At this point we are ready to place the inoculated rice into a warm and humid place where it can grow.

We want an environment between 90°F and 95°F that is pretty humid for the first 24 hours. An ideal way to create this environment is to use a picnic cooler. These are insulated, cheap and come in lots of sizes. The one I use even has a mechanism for heating and cooling. A heating pad or hot water bottles can also be used to warm the environment. Pre-warm and humidify the environment (could start about the same time as steaming) so the rice, once balled up in cloth, will go into a friendly place. An open glass of warm water is plenty to keep the environment humid.

Place a temperature probe in your rice and place in the pre-warmed cooler. A second temperature probe to monitor the environment temperature is ideal but not required. Check the temperature regularly to ensure the rice reaches and remains in the range of 90°F to 95°F. At about 12 hour intervals, open the bundle to check and stir the koji. It may have signs of the white fussy mold by the second check (24 hours) or not. By this time you should remove the glass of water so the incubation environment becomes less humid. The koji will be producing its own heat to the point that you will need to be more diligent about temperature control. Begin 2-3 hour interval checks where you open the bundle and stir the koji. If the koji is reaching temperatures above 110°F you will want to perform these more regularly in order to better regulate the temperature.

From 40 to 54 hours the koji should complete its process. While stirring the koji, you can begin to check it for completeness. Cut a grain of koji in half to see how far the koji mold has penetrated the rice kernel. It should cover about half the diameter of the kernel. Once complete the koji should be spread out and cooled to room temperature. Once at room temperature, koji can be bagged or placed in some container to be refrigerated or frozen depending on how soon you want to use it. If storing for a month or more, freezing is the way to go.

And there it is, are you ready to give it a try?

The Moto

Moto (元), Shubo (酒母), Yeast mash are all names for the Saké yeast starter. Here, I will only use the term "moto" but the three terms can be used interchangeably.

The moto is where the number of yeast cells is increased to the desired level. They can reach 20 million cells in a milliliter or 100 million cells in a teaspoon. The other responsibility of the moto is to provide the needed acid to bring the pH to a safe range for the moromi. Most bugs that might negatively affect the moromi do not do well in a low pH environment. Once complete, the moto is used to inoculate the main saké fermentation, the Moromi (諸味). To build the moto we start with kome (米 - rice), koji (麹), kobo (酵母 - yeast), and today, nyūsan (乳酸 - lactic acid) is often included. These ingredients along with mizu (水 – water) make up the moto.

There are several types of moto or seed mash. There is the currently most used moto type, sokujo-moto (速醸酛), the next most common, Yamahai-moto (山廃酛) and the moto which was king before that, kimoto (生 酛). But, before these there was another type of moto, one that was used as late as 1925 under the name Mizumoto (水酛). This moto was bodai-moto (菩提酛) and was developed by the monks at the Bodaisen Shoreki Ji Buddhist temple. In addition to these there are other types of yeast starters that are less common. For example there is the Ko-on toka (高温糖化- High Temperature Sugar Production) moto that is a high temperature saccharification method that brings the mash to 130°F (optimal temperature for koji enzymes) for several hours before cooling and adding lactic acid and yeast.

Below I will review each of these in detail so you will be able to use the one that most suits the saké you want to make. I am reviewing them in order of their development. As mentioned above, sokujo-moto is the most used moto; it is the simplest and easiest to use. So, I believe homebrewers should start with sokujo and then explore the rest. In addition, the procedures below assume a 60% seimaibuai. If you are using rice with a different level of milling you should make the appropriate adjustment in rice preparation to hit the desired moisture levels. Also, the additions of magnesium sulfate (Epsom salts), potassium chloride (Morton Salt Substitute) and a yeast nutrient below are not strictly part of the specific moto type and can be included or not. I include them here so you can see where I would add them; this is to remove as much of the guess work as possible.

Bodai Moto

The Bodaisen Shoreki Ji Buddhist monks studied the techniques used in both Japan and China. They developed their method some time in or before the 14th century. A brewing diary, "Goshu no Nikki,"[11] describes the two step method and later starting in 1478 as chronicled by the "Tamon-in Nikki"[12] the three step method was developed and used. Taken together, these two diaries describe how the method for making Bodaisen had transformed from a single mash saké brewing method to one that used a starter culture from previous good mashes to one with a purpose made starter mash, bodai-moto. They further describe the continued progress of including two and then three additions for the buildup to moromi. Saké brewing with these three additions is known as san-dan-jikomi (三段仕込み); that is the three step brewing process.

---

[11] The Goshu no Nikki is a technical brewing diary on sake brewing written in the Muromachi period.
[12] The Tamon-in Nikki is a diary that was kept at the Kofuku-ji temple in Nara during the 16th century.

The Moto

Bodai-moto is created by combining raw polished rice, a small amount of cooked rice and water. This mixture is then incubated for around eight days. The cooked rice that is added is first cooled in the open air where it becomes infected with yeast, lactobacilli and other bugs. Originally, after the mixture started to bubble and taste sour, the liquid was poured off through a mesh, where the liquid was used with steamed rice and koji for the main mash. Both yeast and lactic acid producing bacteria were cultivated in the soyashi process and transferred to the main mash with the liquid. This liquid is known as soyashimizu (そやし水- lactic acid water). Current practice uses this liquid to make the starter, moto, rather than the main mash itself. Hiroichi Akiyama[13] says this method of collecting and using the yeast and bacteria is quite stable. However, because it produces such a large population of lactic acid bacteria, it produces pretty sour saké.

The last of those using bodai-moto stopped doing so around 1925. However, bodai-moto was not to stay extinct. A group of brewers from Nara brought it back in the late 1990s and now produce saké with this method. Their experience has not shown the method to be as stable as Akiyama-san states. In any case the following procedure for making a bodai-moto explicitly adds the desired yeast rather than depending on a natural inoculation as do all modern moto procedures.[14]

Bodai-moto Procedure

This procedure for Bodai-moto takes 18 days.

Day 1 – estimated task time 1 hour, beginning the soyashi process to make soyashimizu or lactic acid water:

---

[13] Dr. Hiroichi Akiyama is a former President of the Brewing Society of Japan.
[14] This is not to say that no moto procedure depends on natural yeast inoculation. Some kura do use this method but there are not many that do.

In this section we are making the acidic water that will keep the moto and resulting moromi safe from most bugs that can hurt the ferment. This section has two phases: cooking the rice and combining the ingredients.

Do phase 1:

- Cook rice in any manner you like
    - You will need 4oz. (½ cup) of cooked rice
    - Spread out cooked rice to cool in the open air

Do phase 2:

- Combine and mix the following ingredients:
    - ½ cup cooled, cooked rice from phase 1
    - 2 cups washed, raw milled white rice
    - 3 cups water
- Place in an open area with no cover and let stand for 8 days

Somewhere between days 3 and 8 the soyashimizu will be sour enough to move to the next stage. Here, I will use 8 days. However, the actual day you transition will vary depending on your results. The soyashimizu will begin to smell unpleasant and this smell may become very pronounced.

Day 3 to 8 – estimated time 5 minutes per day

Do each day:

- Check the mixture for signs of bubbling and a sour taste
- Once there has been adequate bubbling and sourness, move on to the next step

Day 8 – Once soyashimizu is sour enough, estimated time 5 minutes

Do:

- Cool soyashimizu to 55°F or lower
- Store at this temperature until ready to begin the moto proper

The Moto

Day 9 – Begin the actual moto procedure, estimated time 1 ½ hours

Do:

- Separate the soyashimizu (liquid) from the rice
    - This may produce a little less than 2 cups liquid
    - The rice may have turned yellowish
- Add water to soyashimizu to reach 2-2.5 cups
- Add 1 cup koji to the soyashimizu
- Steam the rice from the soyashi procedure for 45 minutes
    - At this point the steamed rice is likely red
- Combine soyashimizu mixture with cooled steamed rice (65°F target)
- Add pack of yeast, ½ teaspoon of yeast nutrient, a pinch of magnesium sulfate (Epson salt), and 1 teaspoon of potassium chloride (Morton Salt Substitute)
- Loosely cover with plastic wrap and place where it will not get too much light (target temp: 65°F-75°F)

Day 10 to day 18 – estimated time 5 minutes per day

Do each day:

- Stir well twice a day (use a sanitized spoon)
- Target temp: 65°F-72°F

Day 19, the final day of moto – day before starting the buildup to Moromi – estimated time 5+ minutes

Do:

- Stir the moto
- Begin lowering moto temperature, slowly, down to 60°F

Well, there you have it, the procedure for Bodai-moto which is also known as Mizumoto.

Kimoto

Kimoto was developed after bodai-moto, but sometime before 1685 when it was described in the "Domo Shuzo Ki." Kimoto controlled the level of lactic acid bacteria better than bodai-moto. However, despite the sour saké produced with bodai-moto, the two methods coexisted from kimoto's beginning almost into the present day.

The kimoto method features a vigorous mixing, taking many hours, to produce a puree of the ingredients. It was thought this vigorous mixing, called Yama-Oroshi (山卸), was needed for the ingredients to properly work together.

Kimoto depends on lactobacillus bacteria from the air to infect the moto and create the needed lactic acid. Lactic acid prevents wild yeast and other types of bacteria from getting a firm foothold in the mash which could ruin the moto and the final saké. In this process it takes some time, maybe a week, for there to be enough lactobacillus bacteria and hence lactic acid to protect the moto. Infestations of wild yeast and other bacteria that started prior to the lactobacilli reaching critical mass will be controlled by the low pH created from the lactic acid.

In the standard procedure, kurabito create the moto in eight Hangiri (半切 – half barrel) adding the ingredients to each, mixing them together by hand. On the next day the moto is mashed or ground down with a kaburagai (蕪櫂 - that is a tool with a rounded head for working the mash) three times. After this the contents of every pair of hangiri are combined into one. On the third day of this work the moto in the hangiri are combined into a small tank called tsubodai (壷代) where it continues to be worked with the kai (櫂 – a paddle for stirring). At this point (end of day 3 to day 5) the temperature is lowered to allow bugs to do their thing. During this period nitrate reducing bacteria become active and multiply. This creates the conditions for the lactic acid bacteria to establish their dominance. Soon the lactic acid is protecting the moto from unwanted bugs.

Around days 5 and 6, the temperature is raised to give the yeast a boost. The yeast quickly multiply and begin to raise the temperature on its own. Within two weeks the yeast is producing alcohol and CO_2. From this point and through the next two weeks the main work is related to keeping the temperature of the mash where we want it. Raise it up to a peak and then back down to ready it for use with the moromi.

There is some really nice work that has been done that explains why these procedures are so effective. Let's take a look at what has been discovered.

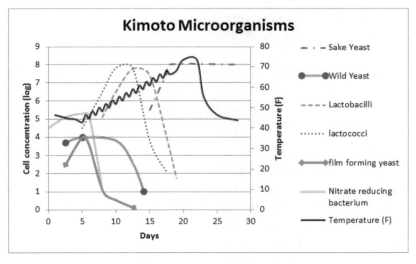

Figure 36: Microorganisms that grow in the moto

By focusing on the progression of time we can better understand what is happening in the moto. In the above chart all the curves represent living organisms except the temperature curve which is controlled by the brewer directly. Very early in the process as the mash ingredients are being combined the temperature is kept low and lowered to very close to 40°F. This low temperature prevents most bugs from multiplying. This includes both the wild yeast and the film producing yeast present in koji at a level in the thousands for every gram. However, nitrate reducing bacterium, like Pseudomonas, are not deterred by the temperature.

The nitrate reducing bacterium increase their numbers a bit while producing nitrite from the nitrate present in the water. The nitrite builds to toxic levels for the film producing yeasts and they begin to die off. About 5 days in, the koji has produced enough glucose to inhibit the nitrate reducing bacterium and provides needed nutrients for the lactic acid producing bacteria which thrive on nitrite and glucose.

Lactococci begin to multiply, followed closely by lactobacilli, both of which begin to produce lactic acid from the glucose in the mash. This combination of nitrite and lactic acid forms the death nail that seals the fate of nitrate reducing bacterium as well as the film producing and wild yeasts. Between days 10 and 15 the lactic acid producing bacteria have produced so much lactic acid that they themselves succumb to its effects and begin to die off. Alcohol from yeast also stresses the lactic acid bacteria to the point of no return. Only saké yeast are left and enjoy the environment that has been created.

It is at this point that the saké yeast present in the moto can be helped to increase their numbers or as is usually done a pure strain of yeast can be added to the mash. In either case the moto continues to be warmed till about day 17 when the heat produced from fermentation is self-sustaining.

The following chart covers the component makeup of the mash for the same period as the above chart and has the same temperature curve to help orient observations as you switch between the two charts.

As you can see, nitrous acid starts to accumulate rapidly around day 5 where you can see the reaction of film forming yeast and a little slower reaction by the wild yeast. Also, as the lactic acid bacteria begin to multiply and produce lactic acid the nitrate reducing bacterium quickly die out. It takes the combination of both the nitrite and lactic acid to overcome the wild yeast.

The nitrous acid quickly vanishes as it is consumed by the lactic acid bacteria and through decomposition as it is not stable in this form. Driven by yeast production, Amino acid levels rise until about day 18 while acidity continues to rise until around day 23. Lastly, glucose which is being created by the koji enzymes from the rice starches build to higher and higher levels until the yeast is added around day 15. The lactic acid bacteria don't use enough glucose to stop the rising glucose concentration but the yeast not only halts the rise but begin to lower concentrations.

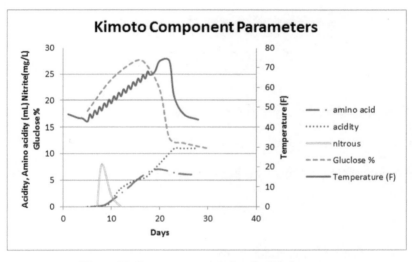

Figure 37: Components variation during the moto

The final stage of the moto where the temperature is dropped and held at a low level is called karashi. During karashi, weak yeast die leaving only the heartiest yeast to propagate to moromi. Traditionally, kimoto has a higher survival rate for yeast through the karashi period compared to the common standard, sokujo-moto. The conventional wisdom for this high survival rate was that kimoto has so much more nutrients needed by the yeast. However, while true, this has not turned out to be the reason. As it turns out there seems to be two reasons for the higher survival rate.

The first reason is kimoto's lower alcohol level which weighs in at around 12% while sokujo-moto's alcohol level can weigh in at 15% unless controlled. The second reason is kimoto yeast have high concentrations of palmitic acid which protects them from alcohol toxicity.

All of the above is for the standard small kura operation. For the homebrew recipes, this process is done twice as fast. The main reason for this shorter time is the difference in temperature between the routines.

Kimoto Procedure

This procedure for kimoto takes 14 days.

Day 1 Morning – estimated task time 10 minutes:

The first thing we must do is to prepare a few things; moto water and koji.

Do:

- Put together your moto water. Combine and stir well:
    - 2.5 cups soft water (distilled or reverse osmosis water is best)
    - ½ teaspoon yeast nutrient
    - Pinch of Magnesium sulfate (Epsom salts)
    - 1 teaspoon Potassium chloride (Morton's Salt Substitute)
- Put this 2½ cup water mixture in the refrigerator and cover

That's it for the first bit of work. From here on, iron free tap water can be used in all cases.

The Moto

Day 1 Evening – estimated task time 3.5 hours, beginning Moto:

This section has four distinct phases: broken up by steeping, draining and steaming.

Do phase 1:

- Prepare rice
    - 1.6 cups of rice
    - Wash and Steep in cold water for 1 hour

Do phase 2:

- Drain rice and place in a colander to drain for an hour

Do phase 3:

- Add 1 cup koji to moto water mixture
- Steam rice for 1 hour

Do phase 4:

- Combine and mix well (target temp:72°F)
    - Moto water and koji
    - Freshly steamed rice
- Mash the mixture with something like a potato masher for 30 minutes
- Place where it will not get too much light (target temp: 60°F)

Days 2 and 3 – estimated time 1 hour in two sessions

Do twice during the day:

- Mash the mixture for 30 minutes. Keep close to 60°F

Day 4 – estimated time 1 ¼ hours in two sessions

Do:

- Cool moto to around 55°F
- Continue twice daily mashing of the moto
- Add yeast to the moto once it has reached 55°F

Day 5 – estimated time 5 minutes in two sessions

Do:

- Allow moto temperature to begin to rise slowly to 70°F
- Begin twice daily stirring the moto

Day 6-8 – estimated time 5 minutes

Do:

- Twice daily stir moto

Day 9-13

Do:

- Lower and hold temperature to 50°F

Day 14 – Day before starting the buildup to Moromi – estimated time 5+ minutes

Do:

- Stir the moto
- Begin bringing moto temperature, slowly to 60°F

And that is it; our kimoto is ready to begin to build the moromi.

Yamahai-moto

In 1909 a modification to the Kimoto method was developed. The modification was to drop the vigorous mixing. As it turned out, the mixing was not really needed. The modified process was called Yama-Oroshi Haishi moto. Haishi (廃止, to cease) so Yama-Oroshi hashi becomes "to cease yama-oroshi." Yamahai takes the two first characters of each phrase, "Yama" (山) and "Hai" (廃) giving the shorter Yamahai moto.

As with Kimoto, Yamahai moto depends on lactobacillus bacteria from the air to infect the moto and create the needed lactic acid. It takes the same period of time for the moto to develop enough lactic acid to protect the moto. So, the standard kura method for yamahai-moto takes as long as the standard kura method for kimoto. As with kimoto, the standard homebrew method takes about ½ the time of the standard kura method. The reason for this is the difference in temperature regimes used. The average higher temperature regime used by homebrewers causes the moto processes to proceed faster. However, the lower temperatures of the standard kura regime will produce a higher quality moto.

Yamahai-moto Procedure

The main and really only difference between this procedure and the previous procedure for kimoto is the replacement of all the yama-oroshi work. That is all the mashing (yama-oroshi) is replaced in this procedure with simple stirring. This procedure for yamahai-moto takes 14 days.

Day 1 Morning – estimated task time 10 minutes:

The first thing we must do is to prepare a few things; moto water and koji.

Do:

- Put together your moto water. Combine and stir well:
    - 2.5 cups soft water (distilled or reverse osmosis water is best)
    - ½ teaspoon yeast nutrient
    - Pinch of Magnesium sulfate (Epsom salts)
    - 1 teaspoon Potassium chloride (Morton's Salt Substitute)
- Put this 2½ cup water mixture in the refrigerator and cover

That's it for the first bit of work. From here on, iron free tap water can be used in all cases.

Day 1 Evening – estimated task time 3.5 hours, beginning Moto:

This section has four distinct phases: broken up by steeping, draining and steaming.

Do phase 1:

- Prepare rice
    - 1.6 cups of rice
    - Wash and Steep in cold water for 1 hour

Do phase 2:

- Drain rice and place in a colander to drain for an hour

Do phase 3:

- Add 8/10th cup koji to moto water mixture
- Steam rice for 1 hour

Do phase 4:

- Combine and mix well (target temp:72°F)
  - Moto water and koji
  - Freshly steamed rice
- Place where it will not get too much light (target temp: 65°F-75°F)

Days 2 and 3 – estimated time 10 minutes in two sessions

Do twice during the day:

- Stir the moto

Day 4 – estimated time 15 minutes

Do:

- Cool moto to around 55°F
- Continue twice daily stirring of the moto
- Add yeast to the moto once it has reached 55°F

Day 5 – estimated time 15 minutes

Do:

- Allow moto temperature to begin to rise slowly to 70°F
- Continue twice daily stirring of the moto

Day 6-8 – estimated time 5 minutes

Do:

- Twice daily, stir moto

Day 9-13

Do:

- Lower and hold temperature to 50°F

Day 14 – Day before starting the buildup to Moromi – estimated time 5+ minutes

Do:

- Stir the moto
- Begin bringing moto temperature, slowly to 60°F

And that is it; our yamahai-moto is ready to begin to build the moromi.

Sokujo-moto

It wasn't until 1910-1915 that there was an understanding of the role that lactic acid played in the moto. Up to this point, the procedures followed for the previous three methods for producing a moto were developed and followed without any understanding of lactobacillus or any other bugs that make these procedures so effective.

With the discovery of the role of lactic acid in the production of saké a new moto method was developed: Sokujo-moto. Sokujo-moto added the direct addition of lactic acid at the beginning of the moto. This resulted in halving the time needed to create the moto, protecting it from wild yeast and bacteria from the start and lowering the final acid levels. Sokujo-moto is the mainstay of today's brewers. It produces a cleaner tasting saké. While Yamahai-moto and kimoto and to a much lesser extent Bodai-moto are still used, they are more of a specialty method used to produce an earthy full flavor saké higher in acid than the norm.

As with the charts for kimoto, the following sokujo chart shows how a few key moto parameters vary over time. The temperature is driven by the brewer while the other parameters come about as a result of the ingredients and temperature. As the temperature begins to rise the yeast start to become more active bringing down the sugar content (measured here in °Baume) while creating alcohol. The yeast also adds to the acidity as a byproduct of fermentation.

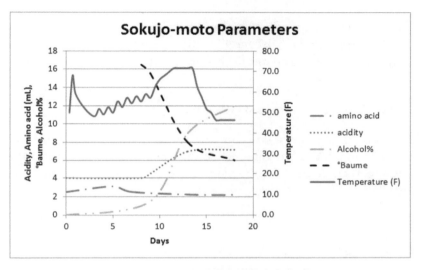

Figure 38: Component variation during sokujo-moto

In contrast to the previous moto methods there is only one bug at work in a sokujo-moto, the yeast. The concentration of the lactic acid added at the beginning of the moto prevent the Nitrate reducing bacteria, the wild and film forming yeast and even the lactic acid producing bacteria from getting a start in the moto. This is why, in practice, this method produces the cleanest tasting saké.

The above chart and its regime are for the procedure as practiced by commercial kura. The standard homebrewer method takes even less time, about one half the time. The main reason for the difference in the time needed is the temperature. The temperature regime given in the chart is quite a bit lower than the temperature regime given in the procedure below and it is this difference in temperature regime that causes the difference in the amount of needed time. Colder is slower. Also, colder is often better, when it comes to making saké. Replacing the time and temperature regime in the procedure below with that of the above chart will improve your saké. The tradeoff between time and quality is yours to make.

Sokujo moto Procedure

The following procedure is the same one used in the chapter "Quick Start Saké Brewing" and is reproduced here for completeness of this chapter. This procedure for Sokujo-moto takes 8 days.

Day 1 Morning – estimated task time 10 minutes:

The first thing we must do is prepare the moto water, yeast and koji. This is done in the morning, while the rice steaming is done in the evening. It could be done the night before, with the rice steaming in the morning, if you would rather.

Do:

- Take your yeast out of the refrigerator and leave on counter to warm (target temp:65°F-75°F)
- Put together your moto water. Combine and stir well:
    - 2.5 cups soft water (distilled or reverse osmosis water is best)
    - 1 teaspoon 88% lactic acid
    - 3/4th teaspoon yeast nutrient
    - Pinch of Epsom salts (Magnesium sulfate)
    - 1 teaspoon Morton's Salt Substitute (Potassium chloride)
- Put ½ cup of this water mixture in the refrigerator and cover
- Put 2 cups (the rest) on the counter next to the yeast and cover

That's it for the first bit of work. From here on, iron free tap water can be used in all cases.

Day 1 Evening – estimated task time 3.5 hours, beginning Moto:

The Moto

This section has several distinct phases: broken up by steeping, draining and steaming.

Do phase 1:

- Smack your yeast pack if you have not already done so and are using Wyeast yeast (White labs yeast does not need to be smacked)
- Ready sanitizer
- Prepare rice
    - 1.6 cups of rice
    - Wash the rice in cold water till water is mostly clear
    - Steep in cold water with 1" water over top of rice for 1 hour

Do phase 2:

- Sanitize the moto container
- Begin preparing the moto by combining (target temp: 70°F):
    - 2 cups of moto water prepared in the morning
    - Yeast
- Drain rice and place in a colander to drain for an hour

Do phase 3:

- Add 8/10th cup koji to moto water and yeast mixture
- Prepare steamer with cheese cloth liner
- Add drained rice to steamer
- Steam rice for 1 hour

Do phase 4:

- 30 minute check of the steaming rice to be sure you don't run out of water in the steamer.

Do phase 5:

- Cool rice after steaming – use the ½ cup moto water placed in refrigerator earlier in the morning
- Combine and mix well (target temp:72°F do not let it get to, or above 90°F):
  - Moto starter from phase 2 and 3: moto water, yeast, koji
  - Freshly steamed and cooled rice
- Loosely cover with plastic wrap and place where it will not get too much light (target temp: 65°F-75°F)

Day 2-7 – estimated time 5 minutes

Do each day:

- Stir well twice a day with a sanitized spoon
- Target temp: 65°F-72°F

Day 8 – Day before starting the buildup to Moromi – estimated time 5+ minutes

Do:

- Stir the moto
- Begin lowering moto temperature, slowly, down to 60°F

Well, that is sokujo-moto; the shortest moto yet. But wait, the next moto, ko-on-toka, takes even less time.

Ko-on-Toka-moto

Ko-on-toka-moto is a high temperature version of sokujo-moto. The idea is that a good part of the time needed for sokujo-moto is waiting for the koji enzymes to convert enough of the rice starch into sugar for the yeast to multiply and put on reserves for the coming moromi. This is slow because of the low temperatures used as compared to the optimal temperatures for the enzymes, around 130°F. So, if we just raise the temperature to 130°F the conversion will go much faster and we can complete the moto that much sooner. However, there is a problem with this. Yeast will not survive this temperature. With a little rearrangement of our procedure we can make it all work out.

First, make amazake by mixing the hot rice and koji together and hold at 130°F for 4 to 8 hours. Lower the temperature to around 70°F and add the same moto water mixture and yeast as for sokujo-moto. Hold this mixture at around 70°F for the next 4 days to complete the moto.

Ko-on-Toka-moto Procedure

This procedure for Ko-on-Toka-moto takes 5 days.

Day 1 Morning – estimated task time 7 hours:

The first thing we must do is prepare a few things; moto water, yeast and koji. This section has several distinct phases.

Do phase 1:

- Take your yeast out of the refrigerator and leave on counter to warm (target temp:65°F-75°F)
- Put together your moto water. Combine and stir well:
    - 2.5 cups soft water (distilled or reverse osmosis water is best)
    - 1 teaspoon 88% lactic acid
    - 3/4th teaspoon yeast nutrient
    - Pinch of Epsom salts (Magnesium sulfate)
    - 1 teaspoon Morton's Salt Substitute (Potassium chloride)
- Cover and put the 2½ cups of this water mixture into the refrigerator

Do phase 2:

- Prepare rice
    - 1.6 cups of rice
    - Wash the rice in cold water till water is mostly clear
    - Steep in cold water with 1" water over top of rice for 1 hour

Do phase 3:

- Drain rice and place in a colander to drain for an hour

Do phase 4:

- Prepare steamer with cheese cloth liner
- Add drained rice to steamer
- Steam rice for 1 hour

Do phase 5:

- Combine the steamed rice with 8/10th cup koji, mix well and hold at 130°F for around 6 hours (finished product is amazake)
    - Stir every 2 hours
- Combine amazake with moto water mixture (target temp: 70°F)
- Once mixture reaches 70°F, add yeast
- Loosely cover with plastic wrap and place where it will not get too much light (target temp: 65°F-75°F)

Day 2-4 – estimated time 5 minutes

Do each day:

- Stir well twice a day with a sanitized spoon
- Target temp: 65°F-72°F

Day 5 – Day before starting the buildup to Moromi – estimated time 5+ minutes

Do:

- Stir the moto
- Begin lowering moto temperature, slowly, down to 60°F

That is the ko-on-toka-moto, the shortest moto I know of. However, there is still a faster way, skip the moto altogether. However, since that is not using a moto, we won't talk about it here in the moto chapter.

Summary

Now that we have covered the five most common moto types let's recap the moto methods we have:

- Bodai, the very first moto method and the only generally known method between the 1300s and sometime before 1685. This method uses raw rice, cooked rice, and water to create a starter liquid
- Kimoto, the main method used from the late 17th century up until 1909, uses a vigorous and time consuming mixing called Yama-Oroshi
- Yamahai, which is kimoto minus the Yama-Oroshi mixing, developed in 1909
- Sokujo, adds an addition of lactic acid at the beginning of the moto and was developed a few years after yamahai
- Ko-on-toka, speeds up the sokujo process by first making amazake and using it along with yeast, water and lactic acid to create a proper moto.

Which method should you use? Beginners should start with either yamahai-moto or sokujo-moto. This is because they are the easiest to master. Yamahai will produce a little more funkiness while sokujo will produce cleaner tasting saké. Kimoto actually produces saké that usually falls somewhere in between yamahai and sokujo on the funkiness to cleanness scale but it is a lot more work. Bodai-moto will produce the most unusual saké of these and is worth doing for this reason alone. Finally, ko-on-toka-moto is the fastest moto to make and produces saké that is as clean as saké made with sokujo-moto.

For those who want to make the very best saké possible it may be worth the extra time and effort to follow the same regime used by the Japanese kura as they make their outstanding saké.

The Buildup - San-Dan-Jikomi (三段仕込み)

This chapter is all about transforming the Moto into the Moromi. After the moto has completed, four days are taken to build up the brew from moto to moromi. The four days are made up of three additions and a day of rest:

- Hatsuzoe (初添) – the first addition, day 1
- Odori (踊) – the dancing ferment, day 2, day of rest
- Nakazoe (仲添) – the second addition, day 3
- Tomezoe (留添) – the third and final addition, day 4

Soe (添 – addition / attachment) is often used for the first addition. Nakazoe is often called naka (仲) and tomezoe is called tome (留). Naka means inside or middle, as in the middle addition. Tome means stop or remaining, as in the last or final addition.

In each addition the amount of steamed rice, koji and water added are increased until it reaches full size after the third addition. At this point it is about 8 times the size of the moto. Roughly speaking, the mash is doubled in size with each addition. The percentage of the total rice bill that is koji generally runs from 15-25% by weight. Of course there are sakés that are made with 100% of the rice bill made up of rice koji but these are exceptions. One other thing that is generally true about the proportion of koji to total rice is that the percentage of koji is higher in the initial additions and lower in the later additions.

Water is generally around 25% more by weight than the total amount of rice. This produces genshu strength saké which should be in the 18% to 21% alcohol range. Additional water added to bring the alcohol level into the standard commercial range brings the water to about 45% to 60% more than the total rice weight.

Anyway, these proportions can be used as a guide to recipe formulation based on the weight of rice used.

Now, generally, these additions assume the moto is the initial mash to which all additions are added in order to create the moromi. However, as I mentioned in the last chapter, the shortest moto or yeast mash is to skip the moto altogether. While this is by no means common, it is done, so I want to cover it here briefly. This procedure is known as kobo-jikomi (酵母 仕込み).

The amount of yeast in a finished moto is close to 20,000,000 cells in each milliliter of moto. The moto is close to a liter in volume or 1000 milliliters. Hence, the moto for the "standard" recipe size used in this book provides 20 billion yeast cells for the buildup and moromi. If we want to skip the moto we will need to provide this quantity of yeast at the start of the buildup. As it turns out both Wyeast and White Labs saké yeast have more than 50 Billion yeast cells in their standard yeast product. Each of these provides more than two times the yeast needed. So we can simply add the yeast along with lactic acid at what would have been the first addition; simple enough.

With the first addition added during day 1 of the buildup, the concentration of acids has been just about halved. This is significant because of the protection from wild yeast and bacteria that the acid provides is now not nearly as strong. Similarly the concentration of yeast is around half what it was at the end of moto. With the start of the additions the temperature of the ferment is lowered. This helps to compensate for the lower concentration of acids and provides a better environment for the yeast. Wild yeast and bacteria do not like the lower temperatures as much as do the saké yeast.

Day 2, Odori, provides the yeast a chance to build their numbers back up to roughly the same concentration they had at the end of moto. During this day of rest for the mash, the yeast are both multiplying (the aerobic stage) and converting sugars to alcohol and carbon dioxide (the anaerobic stage). By the end of the day, yeast concentration has mostly recovered.

The Buildup - San-Dan-Jikomi (三段仕込み)

With the yeast back in strength, the middle and final additions are made on the next two successive days. At each addition, the rice absorbs most of the liquids in the ferment and thickens into an almost solid mash. Over the next few days, the first few days of moromi, the enzymes from the koji work on the rice starch, dissolving the starch and releasing the liquids.

As we saw with sokujo moto, we add the koji prior to adding steamed rice for each of these three additions. This gives the enzymes in the koji time to leach into the liquids of the mash making them available to access the new rice addition. If we do not do this, but rather add the koji at the same time we add the steamed rice, the liquids will be absorbed before the koji enzymes are liberated. In this situation only the koji will have the enzymes and will be going through liquefaction for quite some time before the rice will begin to participate. Only after the koji has significantly liquefied and released its enzymes into the liquid will the rice begin to give up its starches also. This would slow the ferment and may cause loss of efficiency.

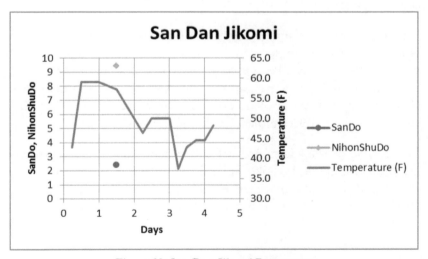

Figure 39: San-Dan-Jikomi Parameters

A typical regime for san-dan-jikomi is given in the above chart. As with the moto, the temperature regime kura normally follow is lower than those homebrewers generally follow. The moto starts around 45°F but the hatsuzoe brings the temperature up to just under 59°F. During odori the temperature is lowered a little to 57°F and then down to 46 for the start of nakazoe. The nakazoe additions bring the temperature up to 50°F. The temperature is lowered still more for the start of tomezoe to 37°F. The tomezoe additions bring the temperature to 43°F. After this, the temperature rises to 55°F for the moromi.

Additions Procedure

In this procedure I use the same amounts of each ingredient given in the "Quick Start Saké Brewing" chapter. The discussion above reviews some guidelines for how to choose amounts of rice, koji and water used at each addition. So, while the procedure below uses specific amounts, you can substitute your own quantities in the same basic structure.

The time spent washing, steeping and steaming should all be adjusted to match the rice you are using and the moisture level you want for the rice. The last variable that you can adjust for the saké you want to make is temperature. The example given in the chart above matches what is often done by commercial kura while the values below are more typical for homebrewers.

Day 1, Soe, of the additions, will differ depending on whether we are preforming a kobo- jikomi or the standard san-dan-jikomi. In the case of kobo-jikomi we will need about twice the initial rice, koji and water as needed for the first addition of san-dan-jikomi.

The Buildup - San-Dan-Jikomi (三段仕込み)

Kobo-jikomi ingredients:

- Yeast with at least 20 billion cells (standard Wyeast and White Labs yeast work well)
- 4.3 cups steamed rice
- 2.25 cups koji
- 5.25 cups water
    - As with the moto, this water should be very soft or even distilled water with the following adjustment:[15]
        - 1 teaspoon 88% lactic acid
        - 3/4th teaspoon yeast nutrient
        - Pinch of Epsom salts (Magnesium sulfate)
        - 1¼ teaspoon Morton's Salt Substitute (Potassium chloride)

Standard san-dan-jikomi ingredients:

- moto
- 2.5 cups steamed rice
- 1.5 cups koji
- 1.5 cups water

Day 1 Hatsuzoe, the first addition.

Morning – estimated time 10 minutes

If you are using a moto, it should now be at about 60°F.

Do:

- Do any needed water adjustment for kobo-jikomi
- Place a portion of the water in the refrigerator
    - 1.25 cups for standard san-dan-jikomi
    - Or 2.5 cups for kobo-jikomi

---

[15] The yeast nutrient, magnesium sulfate and potassium chloride are not required and should be considered only as "nice to have."

- Combine / Mix:
  - Moto if standard san-dan-jikomi or yeast if kobo-jikomi
  - koji
  - remaining water not placed in the refrigerator

Evening – estimated time 3.5 hours

This section has four distinct phases: broken up by steeping, draining and steaming.

Do phase 1:

- Start cooling the mash mixture from the morning to 50F
- Prepare rice
  - Wash the rice in cold water till water is mostly clear
  - Steep in cold water for 1 hour

Do phase 2:

- Drain rice and place in a colander to further drain for an hour

Do phase 3:

- Steam rice for 1 hour

Do phase 4:

- Cool rice after steaming – use water placed in refrigerator earlier in the morning
- Combine the mixture from the morning with the rice just steamed and cooled
- Loosely cover and place where it will not get too much light (target temp: 55°F)
- At 12 hour intervals, stir the ferment for 5 minutes

The Buildup - San-Dan-Jikomi (三段仕込み)

Day 2 Odori

The day after the first addition is Odori, the dancing ferment. This is a day of rest for the mash to recover from the first addition.

Day 3 Nakazoe, the middle addition

Nakazoe begins 48 hours after Hatsuzoe. The ferment should now be about 55°F to 60°F.

Morning – estimated time 10 minutes

Do:

- Combine with mash:
    - 2.25 cups koji
    - 4.5 cups water
- Place 4.25 cups water into the refrigerator to use in the evening

Evening – estimated time 3.5 hours

This section has four distinct phases: broken up by steeping, draining and steaming. This is mostly the same as day 1 with a different amount of rice, koji and water.

Do phase 1:

- Start cooling the ferment to 50°F
- Prepare rice, 6 cups
    - Wash the rice in cold water till water is mostly clear
    - Steep in cold water for 1 hour

Do phase 2:

- Drain rice and place in a colander to drain for an hour

Do phase 3:

- Steam rice for 1 hour

Do phase 4:

- Cool rice after steaming – using 4.25 cups water prepared earlier in the morning and placed in refrigerator
- Place steamed and cooled rice into the fermentor
- Mix well in the fermentor
- Loosely cover the fermentor and place somewhere out of the light where it will cool (target temp: 50°F)

Day 4 Tomezoe, the final addition

Tomezoe, the last addition in the buildup of the Moromi, begins 24 hours after Nakazoe.

Morning – estimated time 10 minutes

- Mix with ferment:
    - 3.5 cups koji
    - 10 cups water
- Place 6 cups water into the refrigerator to use in the evening

Evening – estimated time 3.5 hours

This section has four distinct phases: broken up by steeping, draining and steaming. This is mostly the same as day 3 with a different amount of rice, koji and water.

Do phase 1:

- Ferment should be close to 50°F
- Prepare rice, 10 cups
    - Wash the rice in cold water till water is mostly clear
    - Steep in cold water for 1 hour

Do phase 2:

- Drain rice and place in a colander to drain for an hour

The Buildup - San-Dan-Jikomi (三段仕込み)

Do phase 3:

- Steam rice for 1 hour

Do phase 4:

- Cool rice after steaming – use 6 cups water prepared earlier in the day and placed in refrigerator
- Place steamed, cooled rice into the fermentor
- Mix ferment well
- Loosely cover fermentor and place where it will not get too much light (target temp: 50°F)

This completes the buildup. The next day will be day 1 of the moromi or the main ferment.

The Main Ferment - Moromi (諸味)

Once san-dan-jikomi is complete and the final addition has been made we enter into moromi. Moromi starts the day after the final addition, which is tomezoe. It lasts until fermentation is almost complete. This can take anywhere from 2 weeks to about a month.

The time needed for moromi is based on both temperature and koji characteristics. In particular the characteristic diastatic power the koji can muster at the moromi temperature. The yeast work faster at the low temperatures of moromi than do the koji enzymes.

At the end of the moto the alcohol content was anywhere from about 5% to 15%. With the san-dan-jikomi additions the concentration of alcohol was also cut in the same way as the yeast and acid. However, as some yeast has been reproducing some have been producing alcohol. So by the start of moromi we have regained some of the alcohol concentration we had at the end of the moto.

With temperatures in the range of the low 60s°F moromi may take between 12 to 22 days while temperatures closer to 50°F will take 16 to 30 days. I have seen temperatures as low as about 45°F used for the moromi. The lower temperatures produce more refined saké but lengthen the time needed for moromi.

On day 1 of moromi the mash is thick as the rice added over the proceeding four days has absorbed much of the liquid that had been free. Thick foam that began to rise during san-dan-jikomi continues to rise up from the ferment. Over the following days of moromi as the mash is stirred twice daily and the enzymes from the koji do their work dissolving the newly added rice, the mash becomes more fluid. After day 5 or 6 there is less need to stir the ferment because it is much more liquid and the rising foam has slowed its upward climb.

By the end of moromi, the foam no longer climbs upward. Activity in the ferment slows to be almost imperceptible. It is at this time, somewhere between days 12 to 30 when we should press the saké from the kasu (lees). This process of pressing the saké from the kasu is formally called joso (上槽), informally shibori (搾り), and ends moromi.

Let's look a little closer at the days of moromi. Professional brewers strictly control the temperature of the moromi as they do with the moto and with the three additions, san dan jikomi. As the additions end and moromi begins a typical regime is as follows: Bring the temperature up to around 55°F. The temperature is held at 55°F until day 21 when the temperature is lowered a little before the next stage.

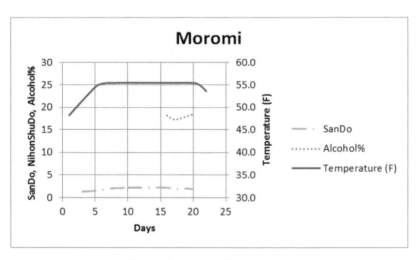

Figure 40: Moromi Characteristics

The acidity, sando, increases somewhat before decreasing slightly for an overall gain of almost 50%. The alcohol content near the end of moromi is close to its final percentage of around 18%.

The Main Ferment - Moromi (諸味)

The stages of moromi can be read by a skilled brewer in the foam[16] that caps the moromi; that is at least when a foaming yeast type is used. As discussed in the yeast chapter for most strains of yeast there are both foaming and non-foaming strains. As the foaming varieties are the traditional strains used, much expertise has been developed to understand the stages of moromi based on the foam or the characteristics of the foam over the days of moromi.

Foam Stage	English Translation	Aprox. Timing
suji-awa (筋泡)	Muscle Foam	day 2-3 of Moromi
mizu-awa (水泡)	Water Foam	
iwa-awa (岩泡)	Rock Foam	
taka-awa (高泡)	High Foam	Day ~10 of Moromi
ochi-awa (落泡)	Falling Foam	
tama-awa (玉泡)	Ball Foam	
ji (地)	Land or Ground	

Table 12: Table 4 Moromi Foam Names repeated here for convenience

The foam progresses from suji-awa through taka-awa and on to ji as the moromi goes through its ferment.

The best description of these foams that I have seen comes from John Gauntner and is as follows:[17]

> "Two or three days into the ferment, small striations will appear on the surface, similar to taut muscle under skin; hence the term suji-awa (muscle foam). Next, a thick layer of soft foam will begin to cover the entire tank; this is known as mizu-awa (water foam).

---

[16] Pictures for each of these stages as seen through the foam can be seen at the Daishichi's site: http://english.daishichi.com/theme_park/sakagura10.html
[17] John Gauntner 2002/03/03 "With foam, brewers call it like they see it" http://www.esake.com/Knowledge/Newsletter/JT/JT2002/jt2002_6.html

The timing of these changes, of course, depends on myriad factors, such as how much the rice has been milled or the tank's temperature. But soon after this, the ferment will enter its most active stage, and foam will rise in great swaths, so that it looks like huge boulders tumbling over each other. This is known as iwa-awa (rock foam).

This continues into the highest stage of foam, known as taka-awa, when the bubbles themselves become very small and fine. This usually occurs around the 10th day or so, but there is great variation.

The foam rises so high that brewers usually use a simple rig consisting of a piece of wire that gently spins on a motor. Its sole purpose is to beat down the foam gradually, which spares them the need for high-walled tanks. It also aids in sanitation, as one of the greatest sources of sake-spoiling bacteria is foam that has dried on the tank's interior.

As the fermentation begins to wane, the foam too falls back, leading to the stage known as ochi-awa (falling foam). This segues into a stage with very large, soapy-looking bubbles known as tama-awa (ball foam).

After this foam also fades away, the moromi's surface is referred to as ji (ground). This stage has many sub-conditions with their own names. Small wrinkles in the surface are referred to as chiri-men (a type of rough cloth). A totally smooth surface is known as bozu, in reference to the shaved head of a priest. If rice solids that did not ferment have risen to the surface, it may look like a lid is on the moromi, and this is referred to as futa (lid).

> Much can be told about the quality of the saké at this stage from observing this surface. For example, if the lid is thick, it indicates that a significant amount of wild yeast ended up in the moromi and survived. This is because the rice fibers tend to attach themselves to many types of wild yeast and rise to the surface when pulled by the carbon dioxide molecules, giving that thick-lidded appearance. Brewers know, then, that a thick-lidded moromi in its final stages will often lead to a saké that is rough, acidic and less refined."

Moromi Procedure

Temperature control is the main focus for moromi. A good practice is to bring the moromi to as close to 50°F as possible and hold it steady at that temperature.

Stirring the mash during the first few days of moromi can also be a good practice to help integrate all the ingredients.

So you like the Honjozo (本醸造)

There is a lot to be said for Honjozo. It tends to be light and fragrant and can be exceedingly smooth. I was ecstatic with the first honjozo I tried. It was the Murai Family Tokubetsu Honjozo, light and smooth, fragrant and then disappears like a ghost; very nice. Since then I have had other honjozos but this one remains one of my favorites.

Honjozo is a Special Designation Saké just as Junmai, Junmai Ginjo and Junmai Daiginjo. In fact Ginjo and Daiginjo without the Junmai designation are both honjozo. You can think about these special designation sakés as having three grades of Junmai (pure rice) and three parallel grades of Honjozo (brewer's alcohol added). The top rung, Daiginjo, is one where the rice used has been milled to 50% or less with one pure rice and the other with added alcohol. The next rung, Ginjo, is with the rice milled to 60% or less with one pure rice and the other with added alcohol. Finally the entry rung to the special designation saké is Junmai (pure rice) and Honjozo (brewer's alcohol added). When this system was put in place, to make this entry rung, the rice used had to have been milled to 70% or less. While this is still true for Honjozo, the milling requirement has been removed for Junmai.

In addition to the milling rate requirement, Honjozo is limited in the amount of alcohol that can be added. This is in stark contrast with Sanzo-shu and Futsu-shu, which, by far have the greatest sales in Japan. The amount of alcohol for special designation saké is limited to 10% of the total weight of the rice used, both steamed and koji.

So, now that we know what it is that we like so much, how can we make our own Honjozo? Well, as you might guess it is very similar to how you brew Junmai saké. The only real difference is that we need to add the brewer's alcohol just prior to pressing. This is somewhere between 12 and 24 hours prior to pressing. The pure alcohol helps to draw out the aromas from the lees during pressing so the end product retains more of the fragrance.

However, the addition of the alcohol also stresses the yeast. At this stage the yeast should already be near the top end of their ability to handle the alcohol. The additional alcohol can push them over the edge causing them to die. Brewers worry about this because the dead yeast may go through autolysis. Autolysis is when the yeast die and degrade; essentially, eating themselves with their own enzymes. They rupture and release their innards into the saké along with off-flavors that can completely ruin the saké. It is for this reason that we don't add the alcohol any sooner than about 24 hours before pressing.

The additional amount of alcohol and water thin the saké, leaving acid and amino acid levels lower than they normally are for a Junmai. While making the saké easy to drink, it can also throw off the balance of the saké if too much alcohol is added. This is of course the art of the addition. Just how much should you add? Trial and error will get you to the amounts that you like the most. However, assuming you want to make Honjozo and not just another saké you will need to stay within the milling rate and alcohol limits as defined. We can calculate the maximum amount of alcohol you can add just prior to pressing.

I will be assuming you are using a recipe similar to the one in the "Quick Start Saké Brewing" chapter. This would mean that you are using about 10 lbs. of rice and about 2.5 lbs. of koji. This gives an upper bound of 1.25 lbs. of alcohol that can be added; that is 10% by weight. 1.25 pounds of alcohol is equivalent to 3.05 cups. OK, so we can add up to about 3 cups of alcohol and still have Honjozo. This all seems straightforward enough; now, where to get the alcohol. Pure alcohol is not easy to come by. A good substitute is Vodka, especially if you are planning to make a standard saké, one that is adjusted to have an alcohol content of around 16% Alcohol By Volume (ABV). An easy to find, 80 proof, Vodka will have 40% alcohol with the rest essentially water. Dividing 3 cups of alcohol by the 40% ABV in Vodka gives the total amount of Vodka needed,

So you like the Honjozo (本醸造)

7.6 cups. Using this much vodka will provide about 3 cups alcohol and 4.6 cups of water.

OK, so what does this do to the saké we are brewing? Normally, after pressing our junmai saké, we will have around 1.8 to 2 Gallons (G) of saké at 18% to 21% alcohol. If we added the above 7.6 cups of vodka and assume that we can retrieve all of it or its equivalent during pressing then we should have the following:

$$Total\ honjozo\ after\ pressing \\ = Sake\ from\ Normal\ Pressing \\ + Added\ Vodka$$

which in cups is:

$$Sake\ volume = 1.8G * 16 cups/G + 7.6 cups$$

or roughly 36cups. The amount of alcohol is equal to the alcohol we would have collected plus the alcohol we added. So, assuming 20% ABV, we get:

$$Junmai\ alcohol = 1.8G * 0.2$$

This is about 5.75 cups.

$$Honjozo\ alcohol = 5.75 cups + 3 cups$$

So the honjozo alcohol is about 8.75 cups.

All of this taken together gives an alcohol level for the pressed honjozo of around (8.75/36) or about 24% ABV. Of course this will need to be adjusted to lower this high level to something more enjoyable; perhaps the standard 16% would be nice.

The adjustment to hit a specific alcohol level can be made at this point or any time prior to bottling. Simply dividing the amount of alcohol by the target percentage will give the final volume that you need. Subtracting the current volume from the needed volume will give the amount of water to add to hit the target percentage of alcohol. Continuing with the example:

$$16\%\ honjozo\ volume = \frac{honjozo\ alcohol\ (8.75 cups)}{0.16}$$

which gives approximately 54 cups.

But the volume of the honjozo after pressing was estimated to be 36 cups of saké. Subtracting these two volumes gives (54 cups - 36 cups) 18 cups of water to add to the pressed honjozo to create a honjozo at 16% alcohol. 54 cups of saké is equal to 3.4 gallons of saké. This is just short of twice as much honjozo than we would have had junmai genshu saké.

```
1 Gallon         ==              16 cups         8.35 lbs water      0.52 lbs water / cup
                 ==                               6.55 lbs alcohol   0.41 lbs alcohol / cup
          0.785 specific gravity of alcohol
          1.000 specific gravity of water
1L               ==              4.2 cups
750ml bottle     ==              3.2 cups
%ABV Vodka       ==              40%             1.27 cups of alcohol per 750ml bottle at 0.4 abv

       12.5 lbs rice + koji (ignore the rice to koji weight and volume differences)
       1.25 lbs alcohol by weight to stay within 10% weight limit for honjozo
       3.05 cups of Alcohol can be added to reach the upper limit of 10% of the weight of the rice

       7.6 cups of vodka at 0.4 ABV to reach the upper limit of 10% of the rice weight, 12.5 lbs.

       4.58 cups water in these cups of vodka
       7.6 cups total vodka needed at 0.4 ABV        ==        2.4 750 ml bottles

Standard Pressing gives:
       1.8 Gallons of pressed sake (assumed)         ==        28.80 cups
       20% ABV for the pressed sake (assumed)        ==        5.76 cups Alcohol

Honjozo Pressing (after adding maxamum Vodka, 7.63 cups, to hit 10% allowable) gives:
       2.28 Gallons of pressed Honjozo sake (assumed) ==       36.43 cups
       24% ABV for the pressed Honjozo sake (assumed) ==       8.81 cups Alcohol

Additional Water needed at bottling to hit target %ABV:
       16% Target %ABV
       2.28 Gallons, beginning Volume                ==        36.48 cups
       24% ABV Beginning                             ==        8.83 cups Alcohol
       1.2 Gallons of Water to add                   ==        18.70 cups Water to add
       3.4 Gallons of Sake at 0.16 ABV               ==        55.18 cups Sake
```

Table 13: Honjozo Calculations with US measures

So you like the Honjozo (本醸造)

The chart above gives the calculations for honjozo using the US standard, while the chart below gives the calculations in standard metric.

The discussion here is all about honjozo and how to remain within its boundaries. However, as homebrewers we may or may not choose to follow these rules. Considerable amount of fine saké is made without regard to these restrictions. Much of the advantages of honjozo will be achieved as long as you don't go too far in the amount of added alcohol. And, in the end, the final judge on how far is too far is you and what you like.

```
        10.0 lbs. rice    ==        4.54 kilograms
         2.5 lbs. koji    ==        1.13 kilograms

        0.785 specific gravity of alcohol
        1.000 specific gravity of water

1L              ==        1.00 Kg Water
1L              ==        0.79 kg Alcohol
%abv Vodka      ==        40%

        5.67 kg rice + koji (ignore the rice to koji weight and volume differences)
        0.57 kg alcohol by weight to stay within 10% weight limit for honjozo
        0.72 Liters of Alcohol can be added to reach the upper limit of 10% of the weight of the rice

        1.81 Liters of vodka at 0.4 ABV to reach the upper limit of 10% of the rice weight

        1.08 Liters water in this vodka
        1.81 Liters total vodka needed at 0.4 ABV

Standard Pressing gives:
        6.81 Liters of pressed sake (assumed)
        20% ABV for the pressed sake (assumed)        ==        1.36 Liters Alcohol

Honjozo Pressing (after adding maximum Vodka, 1.81 L, to hit 10% allowable) gives:
        8.62 Liters of pressed Honjozo sake (assumed)
        24% ABV for the pressed Honjozo sake (assumed) ==        2.09 Liters Alcohol

Additional Water needed at bottling to hit target %ABV:
        16% Target %ABV
        8.62 Liters, beginning Volume
        24% ABV Beginning
        4.42 Liters of Water to add
        13.0 Liters of resulting Sake at 0.16 ABV
```

Table 14 : Honjozo Calculation with Metric measures

Honjozo Procedure

The first thing that you need to do for honjozo is to estimate the amount of alcohol to be added. The above discussion describes how to go about estimating the amount of alcohol or vodka to be added. Once you have the amount to add and you are within 12 to 24 hours of pressing, add the alcohol (or vodka) stirring it in well. From here you follow the same procedure for honjozo and non-honjozo saké. That is all there is to it.

Time for Shibori (搾り)

After the moromi (main ferment) has come to the stage where the ferment has run its course or it is time to stop it from going any farther, it is time for shibori. Shibori is the pressing or squeezing of the moromi to separate the lees from the saké; formally known as joso. This is mainly done in three different ways in kura (breweries) today and probably more ways than can be counted by homebrewers.

The most common way to press is to use a machine called Assaku-ki often referred to as a Yabuta; the name of the main supplier of assaku-ki machines. The moromi is pumped into these machines where it is squeezed by an air bladder to force the saké through a fine mesh that holds back most of the lees. As the lees build up on the mesh more and more of the lees are held back because the lees themselves become a part of the filter. In the most common configuration, the filtering action is so good that it filters out the yeast as well as the lees and hence stops all further fermentation.

Another method used for shibori is to use a fune. A fune is essentially a box with a lid that can be pushed down with great force to squeeze the contents of the box. Bags filled with moromi are stacked in the fune in such a way to ensure the pressure placed down on the lid will squeeze all bags with roughly an equal amount of pressure. The fune has a tap at the bottom of the box where the saké is drained off. The first runnings are collected with little or no pressure applied to the lid; this is called Arabashiri. The middle portion of saké collected from the fune is called Nakadori and is followed by the last portion called Seme. Arabashiri is more wild and brash while Nakadori is more refined leaving Seme as the least desirable portion.

The third method used in kura for shibori is to let gravity do ALL the work. This is done by putting the moromi into bags just like preparing for use of a fune and then hanging the bags to allow the saké to drip. Here, only the weight of the saké in a bag is used to release the saké from the lees while in a fune even arabashiri has the weight of all the other bags stacked on top. Saké "pressed" by hanging is called Shizuku.

Producing shizuku is the most wasteful method but produces the best saké. Using a fune produces saké that is next to shizuku in quality but is much less wasteful. Saké produced with an assaku-ki is still quite good and the process is very efficient.

Having read about the differences in these methods I found it hard to believe that there would be a noticeable difference in the taste of the saké. However, at a tasting of Nanbu Bijin Daiginjo produced with all three pressing methods, I, as many others, found a noticeable difference going from the Yabuta (machine) pressed to the fune (box) shibori to the shizuku (drip) shibori. The consensus at the tasting whole heartedly agreed with conventional wisdom. All versions were very good but the fune version was better than the Yabuta and the shizuku version was better still than the fune version. I was blown away.

Homebrewers regularly use fruit and cheese presses to press their moromi. This is somewhat equivalent to the use of a fune. The moromi is placed into a bag or a cloth and placed into the press. Pressure is applied to the moromi with the press and the saké is collected. This is certainly more efficient than a shizuku style shibori which is also reasonably common. However the time involved for this drip method limits its use. Homebrewers have a third option; hand pressing their saké. This consists of placing the moromi in a bag or cloth and hand squeezing the saké from the lees. While too labor intensive for large batches it works well for small batches.

The shibori bags kura use are made of cotton with a pretty tight weave. Of course the tighter the weave the more lees they will prevent from leaving the bag. Because I hand press my moromi I prefer a very loose weave bag. This gives me a course filtering of the lees that I can do in a 30 minute to 60 minute session. However,

Time for shibori (搾り)

because so much of the lees make it through I have additional racking steps to reach the levels of clarity I want. Basically, I want my saké to be as clear as or more clear than commercial Muroka (pressed clear but not charcoal filtered).

For many first time saké homebrewers, pressing (shibori) is the most intimidating step in making saké. However, as with all other steps in saké making, it can be very straightforward and simple. Even using a cloth, rather than a bag does not have to make it hard. One way to ease this process is to use a large bowl and lay linen or muslin cloth over the bowl making sure that the cloth is large enough to wrap a good amount of moromi and leave room to hold the top. Scoop the moromi into the middle of the cloth and then wrap the sides up and hold the newly formed bag of moromi above the bowl. The saké will drip through the cloth on its own but will take too long for you just to hold it. At this point you can either hang the bag for dripping or help it along by squeezing it. Use your hands or a press if you have one. It doesn't have to be any harder than that.

Final Steps in Saké Brewing

After moromi is complete we have only a few more steps to go in our process. These are: secondary ferment, racking, fining, pasteurization, water adjustments, amelioration and bottling. Conditioning and maturation are also terms for the secondary ferment. For the most part the secondary ferment begins after the saké has been pressed out of the lees. At this stage the saké can be anywhere from milky white to relatively clear. However, in all but unusual cases, more, finer lees will settle to the bottom as the saké completes its ferment and rests.

As the ferment completes, alcohol production ceases but the yeast are still active. During the early stages, acetylaldehyde, diacetyl and esters are produced and cleaned up, however the cleanup follows production by a good amount of time so when there is no more alcohol to produce there is still a sizable amount of these compounds remaining. At this stage the yeast complete their work and clean up remaining levels. It is also at this time that the saké flavors start to come together for a more integrated taste.

Once the lees have settled as much as they are going to, it is time to rack the saké to a newly sanitized conditioning container. A fining agent, like bentonite, can be used to help pull the particulates out of solution and fall to the bottom. In general it will be about 10 days for the lees to drop. Racking can be done ether by decanting or by siphoning. It is easier to siphon from one secondary container to the next without mixing in the very light sediment. Decanting tends to churn the sediments at the bottom requiring more racking steps for the same final clarity.

As long as the saké is kept at 45 to 50°F, the racking process can be repeated several times, with each time removing more of the particulates and leaving a clearer saké. However, with each time some saké is also lost. During one of the rackings, the saké should be pasteurized.

To pasteurize, place the freshly racked saké into a cold water bath on the stove and begin to heat while monitoring the temperature of the saké. Once the saké temperature reaches 140°F take it out of the water bath. This is a pretty gentle pasteurization. As the saké heats up, CO_2 is driven off. This can look like it is boiling but it is only the CO_2 coming out of solution.

At this point there are only amelioration, adding a water addition and bottling left to be done. Amelioration, for those who choose to do it, is similar to the method used for wine and consists of adding a sugar solution (saké sugar syrup) to lower the SMV (Sake Meter Value) to the desired range. Unless the ferment is stopped early, which can result in unwanted by products of the ferment remaining, or a water addition is made, the saké may have a SMV as high as +12 to +16. Most like saké with no more than an SMV of +10; even this is pretty dry saké. To lower the SMV by one point for one US gallon, it takes 0.22oz. (6.3 grams) of sucrose (table sugar). However, it is easier to work in specific gravity. Recall that:

$$S.G. = \frac{m}{m + SMV} \text{ where } m = 1443$$

Based on this we can simply use specific gravity in the formula for the amount of sugar to add for amelioration. The equation is:

$$Sugar(g) = (Target\ S.G. - Measured\ S.G.) * 1000 * 9.5g * VolumeG$$

9.5 grams of sucrose will raise the specific gravity of one gallon by one point.[18] Using a small amount of the saké to create a syrup, makes it easier to mix evenly throughout the batch. Once the SMV is where you want it, it is time to consider a water adjustment.

---

[18] One specific gravity point is the difference in the third position passed the decimal, e.g., the difference between 0.990 and 0.991.

Final Steps in Saké Brewing

Last chance to make a water adjustment to hit your percent ABV target (TABV). If you choose to make this adjustment, you will want to measure the current ABV (CABV) and volume. Measuring the ABV is discussed in the next chapter, "Measuring Your Homebrew Saké." Once you have these three values, the amount of water needed for the adjustment can be calculated as:

$$water\ addition = \left(\frac{VolumeG * CABV}{TABV}\right) - Volume$$

Be careful to evenly mix the water and saké to ensure the consistency of the final saké.

With all the desired adjustments completed, it is time for the final step, bottling. To bottle, rack the saké into its final resting place; these should be freshly sanitized bottles that can be filled to limit the amount of air space in the bottle. If brewing a standard saké, this is the time to perform the second pasteurization. Place the filled bottles into a cold water bath as before and bring the saké to 140°F. Once it reaches 140°F, take the bottle out of the water bath and let cool with the lids loosely covering the top. Once cool, secure the lid for storage.

Valla!

Measuring Your Homebrew Saké

In this chapter I will cover how to measure the key characteristics of saké. These include:

- Nihonshu-do a.k.a. Saké Meter Value (SMV) and specific gravity
- Arukoru bun or Percentage Alcohol By Volume (%ABV)
- Sando or Acidity
- Amino Sando or Amino acid levels

Nihonshu-do or SMV

For Nihonshu-do or SMV all that is needed is a hydrometer. The most commonly available hydrometers are for specific gravity though you can find other metrics. These other metrics were discussed in the chapter: "Nihonshu-do (日本酒度) or Saké Meter Value (SMV)." To simplify this discussion I will stick to specific gravity and SMV.

So, what are we talking about when we talk about specific gravity? Well, specific gravity is a measure of the density of a liquid compared to the density of distilled water at 60°F. But what does that mean?

Let's back up just a bit here. Distilled water is pure water. The distilling process is a means of removing a liquid from a substance by converting it into a gas and then condensing it. When the liquid involved has a boiling point that is distinct enough from that of the other substances involved, the distilling process will separate the substances based on their boiling points. So distilled water will have none of the other minerals, salts or other substances that may be found in water. These, or any other substances in water, will change its weight per unit volume. Also, because water expands and contracts with temperature its weight per unit volume will change with temperature. So to measure a substance's density or weight[19] per unit volume relative to water we need to specify the water temperature and that it contains no added substances. So, we define distilled water at 60°F as our standard and that specific gravity of a substance to be the density of the substance divided by the density of distilled water at 60°F.

$$S.G. = \frac{\left(\frac{Measured\ Substance\ Mass}{Measured\ Substance\ Volume}\right)}{\left(\frac{Distilled\ Water\ Mass}{Distilled\ Water\ Volume}\right)}\ all\ at\ 60°F$$

Because the units in this formula cancel out, specific gravity is a unitless metric.

An easy way to measure the specific gravity of a substance is by using a hydrometer. A hydrometer is a glass float with its units marked on its stem. When floated in distilled 60°F water the value at the point that the hydrometer pokes through the surface of the water is 1.000. SMV can be calculated from the specific gravity by:

$$SMV = \frac{m}{S.G.} - m\ where\ m\ is\ 1443$$

Notice that if the specific gravity is 1.0 then the SMV is zero.

Below is a hydrometer and its jar. The hydrometer is place in the jar filled with a sample of the substance to be measured. The sample size needed is roughly 250ml.

---

[19] Actually density is measured in mass per unit volume rather than weight per unit volume but I am being a little sloppy here. Weight has a linear relation to mass.

Measuring Your Homebrew Saké

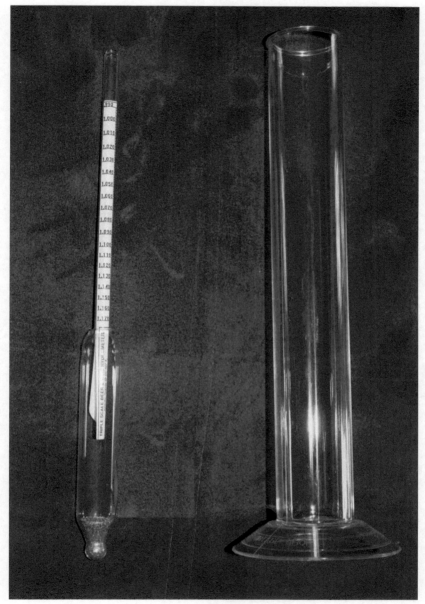

Figure 41: Hydrometer and Jar

To measure the substance it is important to take the reading across the surface of the liquid to the markings on the hydrometer rather than the top of the lip where the liquid rises around the stem of the hydrometer. It can be tricky until you get the hang of it.[20]

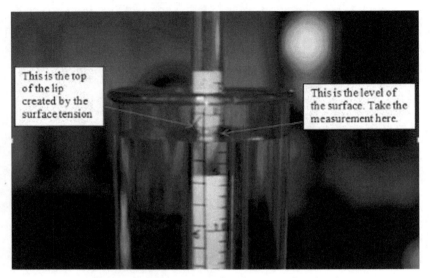

Figure 42: Measurement is taken at surface level

Once you have read the specific gravity you can convert it to SMV using the formula above. Values of SMV above zero represent specific gravities below 1.000 and vice versa. As such there must be something in saké samples that is lighter than water and this is alcohol. Alcohol has a specific gravity of 0.785. So, despite the heavier substances, like sugars, in a saké sample, the levels of alcohol can compensate. Negative values of SMV represent sweeter saké while positive values move towards drier saké.

Well, that is about all there is to measuring the SMV of a sample of saké with a hydrometer.

---

[20] This method of reading hydrometers is the most common calibration. However you should always review the documentation you receive with your instrument to know how it is intended to be read.

Arukoru bun or Percent Alcohol by Volume (%ABV)

Because Heikou Fukuhakkou (並行複醗酵) or multiple parallel fermentation is used to make saké, we cannot employ the same simple method for determining the percent alcohol as is used for other fermented beverages. In particular, the simplest methods used for both beer and wine depend on knowing the initial specific gravity prior to fermentation. For saké, there is no point prior to fermentation when all the sugar is available for such a measurement. Rather, koji enzymes work side by side with yeast in the fermenting mash. Enzymes create sugar and yeast creates alcohol using the sugar; this is multiple parallel fermentation.

The first way to measure the alcohol level we will discuss uses what is known as the boiling method. It is a modified version of the distillation method that can be done at home with relative ease. The basic idea behind this method is that the alcohol in saké has a known specific gravity and a known effect on the specific gravities of substances it is in. Given this we can measure the specific gravity of our saké to get an initial state, replace the alcohol with distilled water and then take a new specific gravity reading. The difference between these two specific gravities can then be used to determine the percentage of alcohol by volume.

The difference between these two specific gravities multiplied by 1000 is known as the spirit indication (A.K.A. specific gravity points). If the specific gravity taken after replacement is SG2 and the initial specific gravity is SG1, then the equation is:

$$Spirit\ Indication(SI) = (SG2 - SG1) * 1000$$

The best formula[21] I have found to give the percentage alcohol by volume (%ABV) is:

$$\%ABV = (0.00803297443 * SI^2) + (0.6398537044 * SI) - 0.001184667159$$

> Note: The following equation can be found on the internet but is incorrect. I mention it only so you will not be confused by it. Please do not use this equation: %ABV = (SI/1000)/2.11*1000.

Jon Musther's site at www.musther.net has an online calculator that will handle the actual calculations for you so you don't really need to create your own if you don't want to.

OK, so that was all well and good but how do you replace the alcohol with distilled water? The way this is done is to begin with the sample of saké, place it in a beaker, flask or other container that can be used to slowly boil the saké to close to ½ its starting volume. It is important that you can precisely return the level of saké to the pre-boil level by adding distilled water. The pre-boil amount should be close to 250ml in order to be able to properly take the specific gravity with a hydrometer. Recall from part one how we used the hydrometer to measure the specific gravity of saké.

Be careful while boiling. Saké, in a small flask, will very easily boil over. It will look like it is not boiling at all and then a series of bubbles will come up the side of the flask and out the top. It may then, also catch on fire. In addition you may have to start over because some of the non-alcohol materials that affect the specific gravity can be lost. Heating the saké up to boiling very slowly will prevent most problems.

---

[21] I got this equation from Jonathan Musther at http://www.musther.net. I don't know where he got it or if he created it but it matches the table values from William Honneyman,B.Sc.,Ph.D. discussed in:
http://valleyvintner.com/Tips&Links/MeasuringAlcohol.pdf.

The reason for using distilled water is to ensure the water being added has a specific gravity of 1.0. If it does not the calculations will be thrown off and you will not get accurate results. Also, to ensure accuracy, the post-boil level needs to be exactly the same level as was there pre-boil. The degree to which you don't get back to the same level drives a difference in the ratio of material that produces a deflection in specific gravity which will throw off the final measurement. If we do bring the level back precisely then we will have replaced the water boiled off with water and the alcohols boiled off with water. Hey, that is it; replacing the alcohol with water.

So, to recap, what we need to do is choose a sample large enough to take a hydrometer reading (SG1) at 60°F, then place the sample in a flask or beaker and boil off ½ the amount, next bring the level precisely back up to the pre-boil level with distilled water, mix and take the second hydrometer reading (SG2) at 60°F, plug these values into the equation above and voila out pops %ABV.

While not overly challenging the boiling method takes a considerable amount of time. A much faster method that is still quite accurate is done using a hydrometer in concert with a refractometer. As the hydrometer uses the relative density, refractometers use the relative speed of light as it travels through a sample medium. The difference in speed between the two medium gives rise to the difference in refractive index.

Many inexpensive refractometers are used for determining the amount of sugar in a solution. They can do this because the refractive index changes with the amount of sugar in solution just as the density of the solution changes. These refractometers often use a scale marked in degrees Brix. Degrees Brix is the measure of sugar in a solution. 1 degree Brix means that 1% of the solution is sugar. A refractometer can be scaled in degrees Brix using a one to one mapping between degrees Brix and the refractive index. Solutions used for producing alcoholic beverages have other components that also affect the refractive index reading so in these solutions the Brix reading is not entirely percent sugar but includes other dissolved solids.

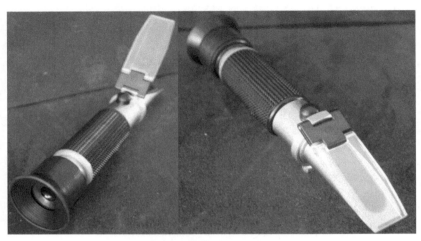

Figure 43: Refractometer

However, the refractive index for solutions that have both sugar and alcohol is more complex. For any given percent sugar plus other dissolved solids, we get a mapping from the refractive index to percentage of alcohol. So to make sense of the refractometer reading we need to know both the specific gravity and refractive index as °Brix. We **MUST** use a hydrometer to measure the specific gravity and then use the refractometer to measure the refractive index as °Brix in order to estimate the alcohol. The chart below shows how a mapping for the refractive index to %ABV for various specific gravities can be done.

Measuring Your Homebrew Saké

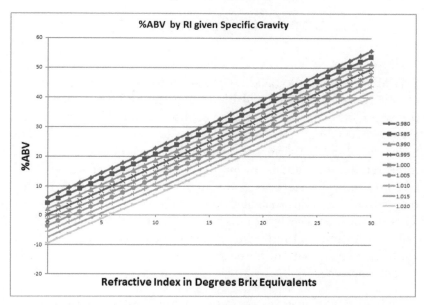

Figure 44: %ABV given S.G. and °Brix from Refractometer

The equation for this is given by:

$$\%ABV = 1.646 * °BRIX - 2.703 * \left(145 - \frac{145}{SG}\right) - 1.794$$

Refractometers like the one in the picture above have Automatic Temperature Correction (ATC). They are used by placing a drop of saké on the plate and closing the cover. You then look through the eye piece and read off the value where the shade changes colors.

After measuring both the specific gravity with a hydrometer and the refractive index (given in Brix equivalents) with a refractometer, plug these values into the above equation and again, voila we get the %ABV for our sample.

Both of these methods work well with the former taking more time and the latter requiring additional equipment (the refractometer).

Sando (酸度) or Acidity

To measure the sando (acidity) of saké at home, there are two very closely related methods available. The easier and less expensive of the two methods is to use a wine acidity test kit. This kit contains almost everything you need to measure the acidity of saké. However, there is a difference getting from the physical test to the interpreted value, but I am getting a little ahead of myself. The second method differs from the first in that a pH meter is used rather than Phenolphthalein to determine the point of neutrality. This method of slowly dripping until the reaction takes place is called titration. Often the second method employs more sophisticated equipment for each of the components but this is not strictly necessary.

So, what do wine acid test kits come with? Well, they come with a small beaker to mix the sample and chemicals in, a syringe to measure with, a solution of Sodium Hydroxide, usually at a concentration of 0.1 or 0.2 Molarity (M) and Phenolphthalein. The idea behind the test is that we have some unknown amount of acid in our sample that we want to measure. To do this, we add a known amount of base to neutralize the sample pH. When we have neutralized the sample pH with a known amount of base we can then workout the original amount of acid. Clear as mud? Let's look a little closer.

To use the kit shown below, collect 10ml sample of saké using the syringe and place the sample in the plastic beaker. Then drip a few drops of Phenolphthalein into the beaker with the sample. The Phenolphthalein reacts by changing color when the sample becomes neutral. Neutral in this case is defined to be at pH 8.2. After thoroughly cleaning, rinsing and drying the syringe, fill it with 10mls of Sodium Hydroxide solution. At this point, slowly drip the Sodium Hydroxide (NaOH) solution into the sample while swirling the sample and watching for the color to change. After a little bit, the color changes momentarily around the drips and then returns to clear. After a bit more the entire sample changes color and the sample remains the new color. At this point the sample has been neutralized.

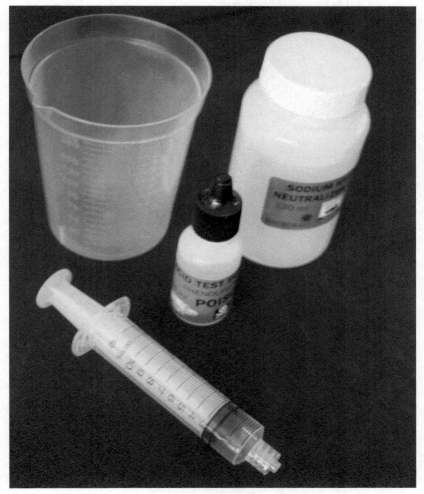

Figure 45: Standard Wine Acid Test Kit

Knowing the syringe was carefully loaded with 10ml of NaOH solution and checking the amount left after titration (dripping the NaOH into the sample), we can determine the amount used. Assume 2ml of 0.1M NaOH solution was used for the calculation below. Plugging these values into the equation for Titratable Acidity (TA) given in g/L of Succinic Acid the general formula is:

$$TA\left(\frac{g}{L}\right) = MoleRatio * \frac{(BaseMolarity * BaseVolume * MoleMass)}{SampleVolume}$$

which, with the above values becomes:

$$TA\left(succinic\ \frac{g}{L}\right) = \frac{1}{2} * \frac{(0.1M * 2ml * 118)}{10ml}$$

or a TA of 1.18 g/L Succinic

Where the MoleRatio and MoleMass will be discussed later, the BaseMolarity is the concentration (moles / liter) of NaOH in distilled water, BaseVolume and SampleVolume are the amounts of NaOH and Sample solutions in ml.

Gauntner[22] puts the range for saké acidity to be about 1.0 to 1.8 with the vast majority of sakés in the range of 1.1 to 1.2.

You may notice however, that this equation is not what comes with the kit. Two main differences exist: acid type and final units used. In saké as we have just observed, succinic acid is used. Succinic acid, along with malic and lactic acid is the most abundant acid in saké. For wine TA levels, Tartaric acid is used because tartaric acid is the most abundant acid in wine along with malic and citric acids.

Two factors that matter in this substitution of succinic for tartaric acid. The first factor is the mole ratio (MoleRatio) for the neutralization reaction. You may recall that a base, something with a high pH value, when added to an acid, something with a low pH

---

[22] John Gauntner, WWW.sake-world.com

value will neutralize, bring the pH value back to around 7. If one molecule of base reacts with one molecule of acid the mole ratio is 1. If two base molecules are required the ratio is ½, and so on. Simply put, the mole ratio is the number of acid molecules over the number of base molecules needed for the neutralization reaction to occur. Both succinic acid and tartaric acid have a mole ratio with sodium hydroxide of ½, so this, while important, does not change the equation.

The second factor is the molecular mass (MoleMass). The molecular mass of succinic acid is 118 while the molecular mass of tartaric is 150. This is the only difference in the above equation. So to convert from acid as succinic to acid as tartaric requires a factor of $150/118 = 1.2712$. However, going the other way would be more natural if you get a TA level based on a wine kit and want to convert the final value. To do this you need to use $118/150 = .78667$ if this where the only difference; however, it is not.

Recall, above that I said the final units used are also different. For saké, grams per liter (g/L) are used while in wine grams per 100ml are used. This approximates a percentage acid to the whole. So, to convert a standard measurement made for wine to one for saké we need to multiply the measurement by $10*118/150 = 7.8667$.

Not all wine acidity test kits give the molarity of the NaOH solution. When this is the case, it is best to use the calculation provided with the kit and then use the above conversion to convert from TA Tartaric to TA Succinic.

The second method for finding the acidity requires a pH meter. In fact, this method is the same as the first but replacing the phenolphthalein with a pH meter. When using a pH meter to determine neutrality rather than a color change, the routine remains the same with the exception of swirling the meter in the sample and watching the meter value. When the value reaches 8.2 we have reached neutrality for this test. Generally a pH of 7 is considered neutral but because phenolphthalein changes color at a pH of 8.2 and this is the standard, 8.2 is used.

Amino sando (アミノ酸度) or Amino acid

As is the case for measuring the sando, you will need some Sodium Hydroxide (NaOH) solution usually at a concentration of 0.1 Molarity (M), phenolphthalein, a small beaker to mix the sample and chemicals in, and a syringe to measure with. All of this can be purchased as a wine acid test kit. In addition you will need some formalin solution. Just as with sando, you can use the phenolphthalein as an indicator or a pH meter to determine the point at which the pH reaches 8.2.

The method used to measure the amino sando is very similar to the method for measuring sando. In fact, it incorporates the sando method as the first step in measuring the amino sando. This is because amino sando is just a specialized acid that is locked up and hidden in the structure. To measure the amino sando we must first remove or neutralize other acids so that they are not counted along with the amino acids. This is accomplished in the first titration step which determines the amount of base require to neutralize the acid. After our sample solution has been neutralized there are no more extra H+ to worry about and we can focus on how to make the amino acids visible, or at least measurable in some fashion. This is done with a formalin solution. The formalin solution reacts with the amino acid freeing an H+ from each amino acid structure. This free H+ can then be locked up using a base just as we did to measure the acid levels. So, one more round of titration using our base solution, sodium hydroxide (NaOH) will give us the level of base needed to neutralize the newly exposed acid, we use this to calculate the amount of amino acid as glycin, the simplest amino acid.

If that seems a bit intimidating, don't worry, we will take it step by step from here.

OK, first we need to measure out 10ml of sample saké to evaluate. Place this in a beaker and add a few drops of phenolphthalein. The drops are not needed if you will use a pH meter. Load the syringe

Measuring Your Homebrew Saké

with about 10ml of NaOH and record the exact amount in the syringe for later reference; call it R1.

At this point, it is time to add, drop by drop the NaOH from the syringe to the sample watching for the indicator to change color to a light pink for at least 30 seconds. Swirl the sample after each drop as you go. If on the other hand, you are using a pH meter, you should gently stir the sample with the meter probe to get a correct reading. Once the color changes and holds its light pink color for at least 30 seconds you have neutralized the sample. Record the NaOH level now present in the syringe; call it R2. The difference between this and the earlier recorded level, (R1-R2), can be used to determine the sando (acidity).

Up until this point the procedure has been the same as measuring the sando. It is at this point that we depart from, or extend, the sando method. Set the neutralized sample aside for use once we have a formalin mixture ready.

Mix 50ml of formalin with 50ml of distilled water. Using the same titration procedure, neutralize the mixture at a pH of 8.2 or where the indicator turns light pink for at least 30 seconds. Remember to add several drops of phenolphthalein if you are using the indicator. There is no need to record the amount of NaOH used for this procedure.

OK, we are ready for the final step. Measure 10ml of the neutralized sample and 10ml of the neutralized formalin mixture and place in a beaker for a total of 20ml. Reload the syringe with NaOH and record the amount contained; call it R3. If you have been using phenolphthalein there should be enough present without any addition. Titrate this 10ml sample plus the 10ml of formalin solution until it reaches neutrality at pH of 8.2 or until the color changes to a light pink for at least 30 seconds. Record the final level of NaOH in the syringe; call it R4. The difference between this and the previous recording will be the amount of NaOH required to neutralize the amino acid present in the 10ml sample; (R3-R4).

Having completed all the measurements, it's time to calculate the levels. First, as before for sando:

$$TA\left(\frac{g}{L}\right) = MoleRatio * \frac{(BaseMolarity * BaseVolume * MoleMass)}{SampleVolume}$$

which becomes:

$$TA\left(succinic\ \frac{g}{L}\right) = \frac{1}{2} * \frac{(0.1M * (R1 - R2)ml * 118)}{10ml}$$

or a Sando TA in g/L Succinic.

And similarly for amino acid:

$$TA\left(\frac{g}{L}\right) = MoleRatio * \frac{(BaseMolarity * BaseVolume * MoleMass)}{SampleVolume}$$

which, becomes:

$$TA\left(glycin\ \frac{g}{L}\right) = 1 * \frac{(0.1M * (R3 - R4)ml * 75)}{10ml}$$

or an Amino Sando TA in g/L glycin.

Where the BaseMolarity is the concentration (moles / liter) of NaOH in distilled water, BaseVolume and SampleVolume are the amounts of NaOH and Sample solutions in ml.

Succinic acid is the most abundant acid in saké. Succinic, malic and lactic acid make up the bulk of all acids present. As discussed in the section on sando, succinic acid has a reaction ratio, MoleRatio, with

NaOH of 1:2 giving rise to the ½ in the Sando equation. The amino acid glycin reacts with NaOH in a 1:1 reaction giving rise to the multiplier 1 in the Amino Sando equation.

The molecular mass (MoleMass) of succinic acid is 118 while the molecular mass of glycin is 75. As you see, these have been substituted in the equations above.

Using a pH meter can be slower and more tedious than using phenolphthalein but the pH meter will be more accurate. In either case, any amount that you are off on any of the titration steps, first for sando, second for formalin or the final step for amino sando, will throw off the following step or be thrown off by the previous step; that is, the error will accumulate with each step.

Another thing that should be understood and kept in mind when working with NaOH is that its concentration will change over time. NaOH reacts with CO_2 in the air neutralizing its base character. You can use Hydrochloric acid (HCl) to determine the strength of the NaOH solution. HCl is stable so, while NaOH is changing, HCl will remain constant and able to measure the new/ current strength of the NaOH concentration using the same titration methods used above.

Well, there you have it, the procedure to measure the sando and amino sando of your saké.

Chemistry behind the measurements – Sando and Amino Sando

A friend[23] helped me to understand the chemistry behind these characteristic saké parameters; sando (acid level) and amino sando (amino acid level). It is not that complicated once the basics are explained but without understanding the basics it is impossible to really know what is going on.

Foundational concept: the mole. A mole is a quantity of objects like a dozen. It allows us to map reactions between individual molecules and atoms and more manageable quantities like grams and liters. One mole of hydrogen is 1 gram. Hydrogen is the simplest and lightest atom with one proton and one electron. The electron weight is so small it is insignificant in comparison to the proton. So the proton as hydrogen itself has an atomic weight of 1. Each atom has an atomic weight, ignoring electrons, equal to the number of protons and neutrons it contains. The neutron weighs the same as the proton.

A carbon atom has 6 protons and 6 neutrons and thus has an atomic weight of 12. Because the carbon atom is 12 times that of hydrogen one mole of carbon would also be 12 times the weight of a mole of hydrogen or 12 grams.

Foundational concept: molarity or moles/Liter. To create a one molar solution (solution of one molarity) of carbon in water simply place 12 grams of carbon in a one liter container and add water until reaching the one liter level. When we talk about the concentration of elements based on chemical reaction equations we do so in molarity or moles per liter.

---

[23] My friend is Jonathan Musther of New Zealand.

Measuring Your Homebrew Saké

Foundational concept: pH, a measure of acidity. The pH of a solution is a measure of how acid or base a solution is with a pH of 7.0 being neutral. Technically speaking:

$$pH = -\log(H+)$$

where H+ is the effective hydrogen ion concentration. A hydrogen ion is hydrogen minus its electron (or a naked proton if you will). The higher the concentration of above 10^{-7} the more acid the solution and the farther below 10^{-7} the more base the solution. While a pH of 7.0 is considered neutral, a pH value of 8.2 is used for titration. Recall that titration is used to find the neutrality by slowly dripping a base into an acid until the solution is neutral. This is because of the use of phenolphthalein as an indicator of neutrality. Phenolphthalein changes color in a solution that reaches a pH of 8.2. Given this "neutral" point is used when using the indicator, it is also used when using a pH meter so that the results will be the same either way.

Now what does all this have to do with measuring the san-do of saké? Well, we can use pH and some basic analytical chemistry to estimate the amount of acid in saké. To do this the first thing we do is choose a representative acid to estimate. This is important because it gives us a chemical compound description and an atomic weight. Given this the more similar the acid is to other acids in the item to be measured the more accurate the estimate will be. The acid used for saké is succinic acid which can be written as SuH_2.[24] For wine tartaric acid is used and is written as $H_2C_4H_4O_6$. Given the acid we can consider reactions that will provide an indication needed to estimate the concentration.

$$SuH_2 + 2NaOH \rightarrow 2H_2O + SuNa_2$$

which is a reaction:

---

[24] Here I am using SuH_2 to represent $C_4H_6O_4$ to emphasize the two hydrogen ions present.

$$acid + base \rightarrow water + salt$$

The two hydrogen ions in SuH_2 combine with the 2OH in 2NaOH to form water while the Su and 2Na combine to form $SuNa_2$ a salt which provides all H+ with an electron to neutralize them. Hence, by using NaOH we can change the pH of our sample in direct relation to the amount of SuH_2 present. So, the amount of NaOH needed to bring the sample to neutral will be the amount needed in the above reaction to remove all SuH_2. This gives a direct indication of the amount of SuH_2 present and hence the estimate we want. The formula used for this is:

$$\frac{C1 \times V1}{n1} = \frac{C2 \times V2}{n2}$$

which says that the unknown concentration of acid (C1) in the sample volume (V1) divided by the molar ratio (n1) is equal to the known concentration of NaOH (C2) times the amount of NaOH solution added to make the combined solution neutral (V2), divided by its molar ratio (n2). In the reaction above for succinic acid, n1 and n2 are 1 and 2 respectively because for each SuH_2, 2 NaOH are needed for the reaction (see the reaction equation).

We can rewrite this equation to give the estimated value we want, the concentration of succinic acid (C1):

$$C1 = \frac{C2 \times V2 \times n1}{n2 \times V1}$$

Recall that concentrations are in moles per liter or molarity. To convert the moles per liter to grams of succinic acid per liter the atomic weight of succinic acid is multiplied by its molarity. The molecular mass of succinic acid is 118. Given this to go from molarity to grams per liter we just multiply C1 by 118 to get the grams of succinic acid per liter. Given this and the values of n1 and n2, our estimate is:

$$succinic \frac{g}{L} = \frac{C2 \times V2 \times 1 \times 118}{2 \times V1} \quad or \quad \frac{C2 \times V2 \times 59}{V1}$$

That is all there is to finding the sando or acid level as succinic acid in saké. Finding the amino sando requires a little more work. As with sando, amino sando follows a similar procedure. In fact the first step in estimating amino sando is to follow the same procedure as that for sando. However, if you are not interested in sando there is no need to go to the work to generate the actual estimate. On the other hand if you would like to have estimates for both the sando and amino sando then collecting the needed information to estimate sando while doing the procedure for amino sando estimation is a trivial addition.

The first step in estimating the amino sando is to follow the same titration procedure as estimating sando. This neutralizes the saké sample so excess free H+ are no longer present. Recall the acid and base are converted to water and salts providing electrons for all of the H+.

As we did with the acid above we need to choose an amino acid to represent the overall amino acids in the sample. For saké, glycin, $CH_2NH_2\,COOH$, is used. Glycin is chosen because it is the simplest of amino acids.

In general, amino acids have the structure $CHRNH_2\,COOH$. Notice that one of the H in glycin has been replaced with R for the general structure. R can be a very complicated structure so it is just a place holder for whatever sets in this position. For example, R is simply an H in the case of glycin. Anyway, COOH is the organic acid component of the amino acid and what makes it an acid. This first titration step removes the hydrogen ion from COOH:

$$CH_2NH_2\,COOH + NaOH \rightarrow CH_2NH_2\,COONa + H_2O$$

As before, this reaction is an:

$$acid + base \rightarrow water + salt$$

but where the salt is an amino salt. So at the end of step one, the interesting component remaining is $CHRNH_2$. Recall that for glycin the R in this compound is simply a lone hydrogen, H, giving CH_2NH_2.

The second step is to add equal amounts of formalin and distilled water. Adjust this solution to pH 8.2. Formalin is a saturated solution of formaldehyde (37% by mass) in water. The formalin solution converts one of the hydrogen atoms in the amino acid to a hydrogen ion. Basically, the following reaction:

$$CHRNH_2 - by\ formalin \rightarrow CHRNH\ H+$$

By exposing the hydrogen ion, the H+, we can now, in the next step, use a reaction through titration to understand how much $CHRNH_2$ is in the sample. This is possible because the amount of $CHRNH_2$ (i.e. the amount of amino acids) is all being treated as if it were all glycin. The number of H+ that have been exposed or released by the formalin is equal to the number of amino acid components the H+ came from. Hence by knowing the amount of H+ neutralized by the known concentration of base we also know the amount of amino acid or "glycin" we have in the saké sample.

In the third step we again titrate with a NaOH solution to estimate the number of glycin molecules based on the following reaction:

$$CHRNH\ H + NaOH \rightarrow CHRNH + Na + H_2O$$

As before we use the equation for estimating the molar concentration, repeated here:

$$C1 = \frac{C2 \times V2 \times n1}{n2 \times V1}$$

However, unlike before, only one NaOH is required in the reaction equation for every CHRNHH+ so both n1 and n2 equal 1 and hence they can be removed from the estimating equation:

$$C1 = \frac{C2 \times V2}{V1}$$

As glycin has an atomic weight of 75 the final equation to estimate the amount of amino acids as glycin (that is the amino sando) in the saké sample is:

$$amino\ sando\ as\ glycin\ g/L = \frac{C2 \times V2 \times 75}{V1}$$

That is the chemistry behind the sando and amino sando measurement procedures. I hope I have been able to explain this in a way that is clearer than nigori.

Sodium Hydroxide Solution Concentration

The last topic in this section we need to understand is how to create and measure the concentration of a sodium hydroxide (NaOH) solution. OK, so you have some Sodium Hydroxide solution that you have been using to measure your saké or wine acidity but it has been a while. Maybe even a long while. You want to make a measurement but will it be accurate? Will it have absorbed too much CO_2 to give an accurate measure? How do you know? Well, with a dilute solution of Hydrochloric acid (HCl), 0.1 molarity is good, you can answer these questions and get back to the task at hand.

Unlike Sodium Hydroxide, Hydrochloric acid is stable so it can be stored and used over a long period without degradation. This stability makes HCl ideal for determining the actual concentration of your NaOH solution.

Using HCl to determine the concentration of NaOH depends on the reaction:

$$HCl + NaOH \rightarrow H_2O + NaCl$$

which converts an acid and a base to water and a salt as we have seen before. This reaction along with the following equality can be used to determine the actual concentration of the NaOH solution if we have accurate knowledge about the other values.

$$\frac{ConcentrationSample1 * VolumeSample1}{MolarRatioSample1} = \frac{ConcentrationSample2 * VolumeSample2}{MolarRatioSample2}$$

Knowing the HCl solution molarity (0.1 for our work) and using a specific sample volume of the HCl solution (say 10ml) along with the fact that the molar ratio in the above reaction is 1:1 leaves only the NaOH volume to be determined in order to calculate the NaOH concentration. Let sample1 be the HCl and sample2 be the NaOH. This gives:

$$\frac{0.1\,M * 10ml}{1} = \frac{Concentration\,NaOH * Volume\,NaOH}{1}$$

so

$$Concentration\,NaOH = \frac{0.1\,M * 10ml}{Volume\,NaOH\,ml}$$

or

$$Concentration\,NaOH = \frac{1\,M}{Volume\,NaOH}$$

Given this, if we titrate to neutralize 10ml of a 0.1 Molarity solution of HCl and it takes 11ml of your NaOH solution to neutralize the HCl then the molarity of the NaOH solution is 0.0909... M or about 0.091 M. Now that you know the molarity of the NaOH solution that you are using, you can substitute this value into the equation you are using to determine the acidity of your saké while following the standard titration procedure.

One additional benefit of being able to determine the molarity of your NaOH solution is that you can actually make your own. With this you are no longer dependent on your lab supply store for

NaOH solutions with an accurately known molarity. The mole mass of NaOH is roughly 40 grams. So to create a 0.1 molarity solution of NaOH we start with 1 liter of distilled water and add 4 grams (0.1 x 40) of NaOH granules. This gets us very close to the 0.1 molarity solution we want but with the accuracy of our equipment it is not close enough. Now, use the above procedure to measure the molarity accurately enough for use in accurate sando and amino sando measurements.

Spoilers and Trouble Shooting

An old enemy of Saké – Hiochi-kin (火落ち or 菌)

An old enemy of Saké and the saké brewer is Hiochi-kin or hiochi bacteria that spoils saké as it grows and reproduces. Unlike most bacteria (bugs for short) hiochi-kin does not mind alcohol and some even like alcohol. So as most Lactobacilli, which are heavy lifters in Kimoto and Yamahai moto styles of saké, will die off as the alcohol levels increase, hiochi-kin does not. The other factor that usually keeps the bugs out is low pH levels like those found in saké which are a result of acids created in or added to the moto. However these hiochi-kin also like low pH, highly acidic environments.

As it turns out, hiochi-kin is a lactic acid bug or more specifically it is one of two bugs: Lactobacillus (L.) homohiochi and L. fructivorans (a.k.a. L. heterohiochi). These are the "true" or "obligate" hiochi-kin and need hiochic Acid (more commonly known as mevalonic acid) for their growth. Other hiochi-kin or saké spoilage bugs are referred to as "facultative" and include: L. fermentum, L. hilgardii, L. casei, L. paracasei and L. rhamnosus.

Koji produces the needed hiochic acid. The fact that "true" hiochi-kin need hiochic acid implies that these bugs are highly adapted to saké production. Thus they have few other environments in which they can grow. Hiochic acid is an intermediate compound in the biosynthesis of many other compounds so it is not normally seen in a stable state (i.e., not part of a biosynthesis process). The chemical makeup of hiochic acid follows.

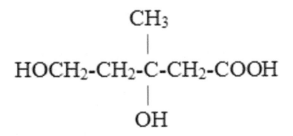

Figure 46: Hiochic Acid (A.K.A. Mevalonic Acid)

Hiochi-kin causes saké to become turbid and acidic. The main acid created is, of course lactic acid, but some of these bugs also produce diacetyl (smells like nasty rubber, butter or butterscotch and may also seem like a slickness on the tongue). When diacetyl rises above our detection threshold in saké the aroma is called Tsuwari-ka.

To defeat these hiochi-kin there have been three methods used. The first method was low temperature "pasteurization" used with an estimated temperature of about 120°F to 130°F. In fact, this process goes back to at least 1568. While the Chinese had been using a similar method for at least 400 years by this time, it is unclear if the Japanese began based on the Chinese method. However, these temperatures were not quite hot enough to do the complete job. In addition, after the saké was treated it was place back into wooden containers which, as we now know harbored the bugs even after they were thoroughly cleaned. So, while this low temperature pasteurization helped tremendously, faults remained.

Going to slightly higher temperatures, 140°F as a minimum is enough to kill these bugs and ensure your saké is safe.

Glossary

Akibare - 秋晴れ - Akibare means "the clear autumn sky" in Japanese, and refers to how saké mellows with time. This is in contrast to Otokozake.

Amakuchi - 甘口 - Amakuchi means sweet flavor.

Amazake - 甘酒 - Amazake is a drink made with koji. It is sweet and generally has only a very small amount of alcohol if any.

Amino sando - アミノ酸度 - Amino acid level for saké.

Arabashiri - あらばしり - Arabashiri is roughly the first third of saké to come from pressing the moromi in a fune. This portion is collected with little or no pressure applied to force out the saké (i.e., gravity alone forces the saké out of the bags of moromi).

Arukoru bun - アルコール度数 - Arukoru bun is the alcohol percentage.

Assaku-ki - 圧搾機 - Assaku-ki is a machine that squeezes moromi to press the saké from the lees. The Yabuta version is the best known assaku-ki; kind of like Xerox for copiers.

Atsu-kan - 熱燗 - Atsu-kan, a term for saké temperature, is "hot hot" (50°C / 122°F).

Awamori - 泡盛 - Awamori is the shochu of Okinawa. It is usually made with an Indica rice (long grain) and black koji.

Bodai-moto - 菩提酛 - Bodai-moto is a moto or yeast mash that is made using the method developed at the Bodai temple in Nara. It is the method that evolved as Saké changed from Bodaisen to what we know today using the San-Dan-Jikomi method (three step brewing method) of brewing.

Choko - 猪口 - Choko is a saké cup.

Chu ginjo shu - 中吟醸酒 - Chuginjo shu is middle Ginjo saké. Saké from the middle of the ginjo grade.

Dai - 大 - Dai means "great."

Dai-shi - 代師 - See Koji-shi.

Daiginjō-shu - 大吟醸酒 - Daiginjo-shu or Daiginjo for short is brewed with rice milled down to 50% or less of the original grain.

Do - 度 - Do means degree or measure or value. This is used as the degrees in a circle or the degrees in temperature. In the term Nihonshu-do, the do on the end is where meter value in saké meter value comes from.

Doburoku - 濁酒 - Doburoku is a farm house or homebrew style of alcoholic beverage made with the same ingredients as saké but does not qualify as Seishu - 清酒 - the official Japanese name for saké.

Fukurozuri - 袋吊り - Fukurozuri is a method to separate the saké from the lees where by the saké is left to drip from bags of moromi lees with no pressure applied; letting gravity do all the work. This method is used for only the best saké.

Fune - 槽 - Fune is a box used to press the moromi to separate the saké from the kasu (lees). This kanji character can also be pronounced as "So."

Futa - 蓋 - Futa means lid but in the koji making context it is used to refer to the small boxes koji is incubated in during the second half of the koji making process.

Glossary

Futakojiho - 蓋麹法 - Futakojiho is the traditional method of mixing koji in a box or futa and rotating the position of the boxes in the stack to equalize the temperature of the koji.

Futsu-shu - 普通酒 - Normal saké with no special grade or moniker.

Genryomai - 原料米 - Genryomai is a rice variety used to make saké. This term may be found on saké labels.

Genshu - 原酒 - Genshu saké is saké that has not been diluted by adding water as most sakés are. Genshu sakés are normally from 18% to 21% alcohol.

Genzairyo - 原材料 - Genzairyo is "ingredients" on saké labels.

Ginjo-shu - 吟醸酒 - Ginjo-shu or Ginjo for short is saké brewed with rice milled down to 60% or less of the original grain.

Go - 合 - Go is a unit of volumetric measure that is equal to 180ml. It is also the standard size for the amount a Masu - 枡 - will hold.

Hana-bie - 花冷え - Hana-bie, a term for saké temperature, is "Flower chilled" (10°C / 50°F).

Hangiri - 半切 - Hangiri is the half cut barrel used for making kimoto. It is a wide container with a flat bottom which helps with yama-oroshi or the mashing of the mixture between the bottom of the hangiri and the kai paddle.

Hatsuzoe - 初添 - This is the first addition of koji, rice and water to the moto while building up to Moromi, the main ferment.

Heikou Fukuhakkou - 並行複醗酵 - Heikou fukuhakkou is multiple parallel fermentation. It consists of koji enzymes converting rice starches to sugar (mostly glucose) and yeast converting the sugar to alcohol and carbon dioxide all at the same time.

Hi-ire - 火入れ – See Pasteurization.

Hi-ochi - 火落ち - Hi-ochi is the sweet, yeasty, funky, unpleasant way namazake gets when it has gone bad.

Hinata-kan - 日向燗 - Hinata-kan, a term for saké temperature, is "Out in the sun hot" (30°C / 86°F).

Hitohada-kan - 人肌燗 - Hitohada-kan, a term for saké temperature, is "A person's skin hot" (35°C / 95°F).

Hiya Oroshi - ひやおろし - Hiya Oroshi is saké that is pasteurized before storage and not at bottling. So it is only pasteurized once. In contrast regular saké is pasteurized twice and Namazake is unpasteurized.

Ho - 法 - Ho means method.

Honjozo - 本醸造 - Honjozo is saké with rice milled to 70% or less of its original weight and has a small amount of brewers alcohol added to open up the flavor and aroma.

Honkaku - 本格 - shochu: Honkaku means authentic or "classical method" shochu. Honkaku is the new term for otsurui shochu, which means "second rank", but because this legal designation is confusing Honkaku is used. Essentially, Honkaku is shochu that has been distilled only once so it retains more of the natural flavors and aromas.

Ichi koji, ni moto, san tsukuri - 一麹二もと三造り - Ichi koji, ni moto, san tsukuri is a common saying of many saké brewers. It means first koji, second moto, third moromi. This is the order of importance of their impact on the quality of saké.

Imo - 芋 - Imo is a sweet potato.

Imojōchū - 芋焼酎 - Imo (sweet potato) shochu or shochu made with sweet potato.

Glossary

Iwa-awa - 岩泡 - Iwa-awa is "rock foam," a description of the foam of the moromi that follows the mizu-awa stage. See: Moromi Foam.

Izakaya - 居酒屋 - Izakaya is a small tapas pub. That is a pub that serves food tapas style.

Ji - 地 - Ji is "land," a description of the final foam stage of the moromi that follows the tama-awa stage. See: Moromi Foam.

Jizake - 地酒 - Jizake is saké from small, local kura.

Jo - 上 - Jo is on top or above. It is also read / spoken as "Ue." Jo - 上 - is the first syllable Joso.

Jo - 醸 - Jo is brew or ferment.

Jo-kan - 上燗 - Jo-kan, is a term for saké temperature, is "upper hot" (45°C / 113°F).

Jo-on - 常温 - Jo-on, a term for saké temperature, is "normal room temperature" (20°C / 68°F).

Joso - 上槽 - Joso is to press the moromi to extract the saké from the lees. The two kanji mean "above" and "fune."

Jozo - 醸造 - Jozo means brewing or to brew.

Junmai-shu - 純米酒 - Junmai-shu is saké made with only rice, koji, yeast and water. Specifically no brewers alcohol is added.

Kaburagai - 蕪櫂 - Kaburagai is a tool used for mashing and grinding the rice and koji while making a moto in the kimoto style. It has a long handle and a flattish bottom to smash the rice and koji between itself and the bottom.

Kai - 櫂 - Kai is a paddle used to stir the moto and / or moromi.

Kai-ire - 櫂入れ - Kai-ire is the process of stirring the mash with a kai (paddle).

Kakemai - 掛米 - Kakemai is the adjunct rice added to both the moto and the moromi along with the koji. The combination of koji and kakemai make up the total rice volume for the saké brew.

Kan-zukuri - 寒作り - This is the traditional method of saké brewing in which the saké is fermented cold, in the range of 45°F to 55°F. It is the dominate, maybe exclusive method for brewing saké today.

Kanzake - 燗酒 - Kanzake is warmed saké.

Karakuchi - 辛口 - Karakuchi means dry seeming or dry flavor.

Kasu - 粕 - The lees remaining after the saké has been removed from a saké ferment.

Ki - 黄 - Ki is yellow.

Ki-kōjikin - 黄麹 - Ki-koji-kin is yellow koji-kin or Aspergillus Oryzae. This is the koji-kin used almost exclusively for saké.

Kijoshu - 貴醸酒 - Kijoshu is saké made with saké. That is about half of the water normally used for a batch of saké is replaced with saké. This results in a sweet saké, usually aged for a few years before use.

Kikizake - 利き酒 - Kikizake is saké tasting.

Kimoto - 生酛 - Kimoto is generally considered the original method for creating a saké yeast mash or starter. This method, often considered the only method up until 1909. However, this ignores Bodai moto. Kimoto is different from more modern methods in that it required the mixing of the mash until the rice was completely pureed.

Glossary

Ko-on toka - 高温 糖化 - moto: Ko-on (high temperature) toka (conversion to sugar) moto is a modification of Sokujo moto where steamed rice and koji are initially combined and held at 130°F to convert starch to sugar before adding lactic acid and yeast.

Kobo - 酵母 - Kobo is the "mother of fermentation" i.e., yeast.

Koji - 麹 - Koji or Kome-koji is steamed rice that has been used as the base for culturing Aspergillus Oryzae. A. Oryzae covers the rice as a white fuzzy mold and produces enzymes which break down the starch and proteins in the rice.

Koji Muro - 麹室 - Koji Muro is the room for making koji or koji making room.

Koji-kin - 麹菌 - Koji-kin is koji that has gone to spore. It is also known as Aspergillus Oryzae.

Koji-shi - 麹師 - Koji-shi is the chief koji maker in a kura. Dai-shi - 代師 - is another name for this. The koji-shi in a kura is commonly called Koji-ya-san - 麹屋さん

Koji-ya-san - 麹屋さん - See Koji-shi.

Kome - 米 - Rice that has not been cooked.

Komejōchū - 米焼酎 - Komejochu is rice shochu or shochu made from rice.

Korui - 甲類 - shochu: This is a shochu that is distilled several times and is most like vodka. Sometimes it is simply called kōshu - 甲酎. Shochu distilled only once is called Otsurui.

Koshiki - 甑 - Koshiki is a large steaming vessel for rice steaming.

Koshu - 古酒 - Koshu is saké that has been aged no less than two to three years.

Kuchikami no saké - 口噛みの酒 - Kuchikami no saké is literally "mouth-chewed saké;" a very old alcoholic beverage that uses the enzymes in saliva to convert starch into sugar. Once sugar is present yeast can act on it to make alcohol.

Kura - 蔵 - Kura or Sakagura is a saké brewery.

Kurabito - 蔵人 - Kurabito is literally 'brewery-people.' Those who work in the kura.

Kuramoto - 蔵元 - Kuramoto is the head of the kura. Kuramoto is seldom the Toji.

Kuro - 黒 - Kuro is black or dark.

Kurokōjikin - 黒麹菌 - Kuro-kōji-kin it the Black Koji-kin or Aspergillus Awamori.

Kuroshu - 黒酒 - Kuroshu is saké using unpolished (brown) rice.

Masu - 枡 - Masu is the square measuring box which holds 1 go (180ml) that is also used for serving and drinking saké.

Meigara - 銘柄 - Meigara is the brand name of a saké. This term can be found on saké labels.

Miyamizu - 宮水 - This is the heavenly water from the Nada area used to make saké.

Mizu-awa - 水泡 - Mizu-awa is "water foam," a description of the foam of the moromi that follows the suji-awa stage. See: Moromi Foam.

Mizu-Moto - 水もと - Mizu-moto is another name for bodai-moto. It refers to the water (Mizu) that results from the process having gained a sufficient amount of lactic acid to control the population of other bugs in the moto and prevent them from harming the moto.

Glossary

Moromi - 諸味 - Moromi is the main fermentation of a saké batch.

Moromi Foam - 諸味泡 - Moromi foam refers to the different types of foam that occur and show progress through the stages of moromi, the main fermentation. They include: suji-awa - 筋泡 - Muscle Foam day 2-3 of Moromi, mizu-awa - 水泡 - Water Foam, iwa-awa - 岩泡 - Rock Foam, taka-awa - 高泡 - High Foam About day 10 of Moromi, ochi-awa - 落泡 - Falling Foam, tama-awa - 玉泡 - Ball Foam, and ji - 地 - Land or Ground.

Moto - 元 - Moto is the yeast starter or yeast mash for a batch of saké. Also called shubo.

Moyashi - もやし - Moyashi are sprouts. When written on signboards vertically, this indicates a supplier of koji for saké brewers. This is because koji look like they have sprouts at the micro level.

Mugi - 麦 - Mugi is a broad term for cereal grains.

Mugijōchū - 麦焼酎 - Mugijocho is Mugi shochu or shochu made with Mugi.

Muroka - 無濾過 - Muroka is saké that has not gone through charcoal filtering. This is saké that has been pressed clear (unlike Nigori, does not have kasu left in the saké) but will show some material dropping out of solution over time.

Nakazoe - 仲添 - Nakazoe is the second or middle addition of koji, rice and water added to the moto during the buildup to Moromi, the main ferment.

Nama - 生 - Nama saké is unpasteurized saké, also written as namazake. Nama saké may contain live yeast, bacteria and active enzymes that continue to operate on the saké and change its characteristics.

Nama Chozo - 生貯蔵 - Nama Chozo is saké that has only been pasteurized once at bottling. This is in contrast with both Nama which is unpasteurized and regular saké which is usually pasteurized twice.

Namazake - 生酒 - Namazake is unpasteurized saké. Also known as nama saké.

Nigorizake - 濁り酒 - Nigorizake or simply nigori is a lightly filtered saké that remains cloudy and sweet. The bottle is usually shaken to incorporate the sediments before pouring a glass.

Nihonshu - 日本酒 - Japanese Saké is broadly Japanese alcohol or narrowly the refined Japanese alcoholic drink made with rice, koji, yeast and water. The first two letters are for Japan i.e., Nihon - 日本 - and the last letter is for alcoholic drink i.e., Shu - 酒 -. Shu is also pronounced saké.

Nihonshu no Hi - 日本酒の日 - Nihonshu no Hi is Saké day, October 1.

Nihonshu-do - 日本酒度 - This is the same as the Saké Meter Value (SMV) and relates to the specific gravity of the saké. A value of zero equals the specific gravity of 1.0; the greater value, the lower the specific gravity and the dryer the saké. The more negative the value, the higher the specific gravity and the sweeter the saké. For example a -4 is a pretty sweet saké while a +10 is an extremely dry saké.

Nomi-dachi - 飲達 - Nomi-dachi is drinking friends. I don't know the original source but Saké-Nomi (A Saké only store in Seattle) uses this term liberally :-).

Nuka - 糠 - Nuka is the rice bran that is removed during rice milling or polishing.

Nuru-kan - ぬる燗 - Nuru-kan, a term for saké temperature, is "warm hot" (40°C / 104°F).

Glossary

Ochi-awa - 落泡 - Ochi-awa is "falling foam," a description of the foam of a stage of the moromi that follows the taka-awa stage. See: Moromi Foam.

Odori - 踊 - "The dancing ferment." Odori is the day after Hatsuzoe and before Nakazoe during the buildup to moromi. Odori is a day of rest for the ferment, or at least having no additions.

Otokozake - 男酒 - Otokozake means "men's saké" referring to the strong bite and deep flavor. This name was given to fresh saké from Nada.

Otsurui - 乙類 - shōchū: This is "second rank" shochu meaning that it has not gone through as many distillations as Korui "first rank" shōchū. Because of confusion of ranks with quality this is now mostly called Honkaku shochu.

Pasteurization: Pasteurization is the process by which we kill off most of the bacteria, yeasts and such that are alive in whatever we are pasteurizing. I pasteurize my saké by putting it in a bath of water and bringing the saké up to a temperature of 140°F and intermediately removing it from the heat. However, times and temperatures vary.

Reishu - 冷酒 - Reishu is child saké.

Sakagura - 酒蔵 - Sakagura or kura is a saké brewery.

Sakamai - 酒米 - Sakamai is rice specifically developed or used for making saké. Shokumai is rice for eating.

Sakazuki - 杯 - Sakazuki is a saké cup.

Saké - 酒 - See Nihonshu.

San-Dan-Jikomi - 三段仕込み - San-Dan-Jikomi is the three step brewing method. Also, written and pronounced as san-dan-shikomi.

It refers to adding koji, rice and water in three separate steps to convert the moto into the moromi.

Sando - 酸度 - Sando is the acidity level. For saké the sando tends to be between 0.8 and 1.7. This value represents the concentration of acid (assuming it is succinic acid) in grams per liter.

Sanzo-shu - 三増酒 - Sanzo-shu is triple saké or saké that has been tripled in quantity by adding brewers alcohol. This practice started in the 1940s in Manchuria which had dire shortages. Sanzo-shu makes up most the volume of saké produced.

Seimai - 精米 - Seimai is rice polishing or rice milling. This is the process of polishing, milling or grinding away the outer surface of the rice.

Seimaibuai - 精米歩合 - The degree to which the rice is polished. For example, a 60% Seimaibuai is rice polished down to where 60% of the original rice remains.

Seimaijo - 精米所 - Seimaijo is a small automated rice mill where farmers with small rice harvests can mill their own rice. A site with nice pictures of a seimaijo is:

 http://slurplog.blogsome.com/2006/11/10/kumamotoglorious-rice/

Seishu - 清酒 - The official Japanese name for saké.

Seizo nengetsu - 製造年月 - Seizo nengetsu is the bottling date for the saké.

Shibori - 搾り - Shibori is to press or squeeze. This is the stage where the lees are pressed from the moromi or main ferment. It is also called Joso.

Shiboritate - 搾立て - Shiboritate is freshly pressed saké that is shipped without the normal conditioning period of around six months.

Shinpaku - 心白 - Shinpaku, "White Heart," is the soft white opaque center of a sakemai or rice specifically for making saké. This rice tends to be larger and softer than shokumai or rice specifically for eating.

Shinseki - 浸漬 - Shinseki is steeping, a process of soaking the rice to ready it for steaming.

Shinshu - 新酒 - Shinshu is new saké that generally has not been aged like regular saké (i.e., aged for 3-6 months).

Shiro - 白 - Shiro is white.

Shirokōjikin - 白麹菌 - Shiro-koji-kin is the white koji-kin, Aspergillus Kawachi, named after the man who noticed and separated this mutation from kuro-kōji-kin or black koji-kin in the 1920s.

Shirozake - 白酒 - Shirozake is a sweet white saké like drink made by combining rice, koji and shochu to form a liquor. To make shirozake the rice is steamed and mixed with koji and shochu and then left to age for a month. Once aged the mixture is puréed into a consistently smooth drink about 45% rice extracts and having 8-9% alcohol.

Shiyo kobo - 使用酵母 - Shiyo kobo is the yeast variety used in the saké. This term is found on saké labels.

Shizukazake - 雫酒 - Shizukazake is saké made by letting the saké drip from bags of moromi kasu (the fermentation lees) rather than pressing bags to filter the saké from the lees. This method is mostly used for the highest quality saké.

Shizuku - 雫 - Shizuku is saké that was collected from hanging bags of moromi dripping their contents.

Shochu - 焼酎 - Shochu (meaning "burning saké") is a traditional Japanese distilled drink. Shochu can be made with any of a variety of starches. Koji is used to convert the starch into sugars that can be fermented. Popular starches include: rice, sweet potato and buckwheat.

Shokumai - 食米 - Shokumai is rice made for eating. This is not Sakemai (or rice made for saké making).

Shu - 酒 - Shu and Saké are two different pronunciations for the same Chinese character 酒.

Shubo - 酒母 - Shubo is the yeast starter or yeast mash for a batch of saké. Also called the moto.

Shuzo - 酒造 - Shuzo is brewing or sometimes brewery. It is often used in the name of companies to indicate they are breweries.

Soba - 蕎麦 - Soba is the Japanese word for buckwheat.

Sobajōchu - そば焼酎 - Sobajochu is shochu made from soba. For some reason そば焼酎 is common while 蕎麦焼酎 is not despite the former mixing hiragana and kanji.

Soju - 소주 - Soju is a Korean distilled drink.

Sokujō - 速醸 - Sokujo is the most modern method for a yeast mash or starter. Sokujo is the successor to the yamahai method. Lactic acid is added at the start of the mash to protect it from bacteria. This also halves the time needed for the mash. Earlier methods, bodai, kimoto and yamahai, naturally cultured lactobacillus bacteria to provide the needed lactic acid.

Soyashi - そやし - process: Soyashi process is the process used to make soyashimizu, the special water used in bodai-moto. The process consists of combining a small amount of cooked rice with raw rice and water and left for several days to develop an adequate amount of lactic acid and sometimes yeast.

Glossary

Soyashimizu - そやし水 - Soyashimizu is the water (mizu) created in the soyashi process. This is the process used to create the special water for bodai-moto.

Suji-awa - 筋泡 - Suji-awa is "muscle foam," a description of the foam of the moromi after a few days. See: Moromi Foam.

Suzu-bie - 涼冷え - Suzu-bie, a term for saké temperature, is "cool chilled" (15°C / 59°F).

Taka-awa - 高泡 - Taka-awa is "high foam," a description of the foam of the moromi that follows the iwa-awa stage. See: Moromi Foam.

Tama-awa - 玉泡 - Tama-awa is "ball foam," a description of the foam of a stage of the moromi that follows the ochi-awa stage. See: Moromi Foam.

Taru - 樽 - Taru is a wood cast for storing saké. Kind of like a small barrel or keg.

Taruzake - 樽酒 - Taruzake is saké that has been aged in casts so it takes on the fragrance of the wood.

Taue - 田植 - Taue is rice planting. Rice is first grown in a green house or such and then planted / transplanted into a rice paddy.

Tei-seihaku-shu - 低精白酒 - Tei-seihaku-shu is saké with a high seimai buai (rice milling ratio), for example 80%. One reason for using such lightly milled rice is to preserve the pure rice flavors and aromas.

Titration – Titration is the process of slowly adding a base solution to an acid sample until the sample's pH has been neutralized.

Tobikiri-kan - 飛び切り燗 - Tobikiri-kan, a term for saké temperature, is "fly away for good" hot saké. (55°C / 131°F)

Tobin - 斗瓶 - Tobin is a bottle which holds 1 To, 100 go or the equivalent of 18 liters.

Tobingakoi - 斗瓶囲い - Tobingakoi is saké that is pressed into tobin (bottles holding 1 To = 18 liter). The Toji can then select from the tobin the best of the best saké with the best tobin being roughly from the middle of the pressing.

Toji - 杜氏 - The head brewer at a kura (saké brewery); a master saké brewer.

Toji Mei - 杜氏名 - Toji Mei is the name of the toji and used on bottles to indicate where the Toji's name should be.

Tokubetsu - 特別 - Tokubetsu is a special designation that indicates the saké is somehow special and applies to the Honjozo and Junmai class of saké. It is sometimes used for Ginjo class saké but has no official meaning when used in this context.

Tokutei meishō-shu - 特定名称酒 - Tokutei meishō-shu is "special designation saké," which is premium sakés distinguished by the degree to which the rice is polished and whether brewer's alcohol has been added or not.

Tomezoe - 留添 - Tomezoe is the third and final addition of koji, rice and water added to the moto during the buildup to moromi, the main ferment.

Tomo-dachi - 友達 - Tomo-dachi means a friend or friends. Dachi itself means friend but is very informal.

Tsubodai - 壺代 - Tsubodai is a small tank used for the moto.

Yamahai - 山廃 - Yamahai is a refinement of the kimoto method for creating a yeast mash or starter. The yamahai method does not puree the mash but adds a little more liquid and takes a little more time to complete.

Glossary

Yamaoroshi - 山卸 - Yamaoroshi is the process used to pulverize rice and koji into a paste while performing a kimoto style moto.

Yamaoroshi haishi - 山卸 廃止 - Yama-oroshi haishi is to discontinue the yama-oroshi process. That is not to pulverize the moto mash into a paste. This is the original, long, phrase for the Yamahai method. Notice that Yamahai just takes the first character from each word; 山 and 廃.

Yeast - 酵母 - Yeast or kobo is a microorganism that metabolizes sugars, producing equal parts alcohol and carbon dioxide. Yeast also produces many other compounds, flavors and esters.

Yodan - 四段 - Yodan is the fourth addition. When performed it is done near the end of moromi. Water, koji and rice may be added to adjust the saké. The yodan addition is seldom done.

Yon-gō bin - 四合瓶 - Yon-go bin literally means 4 Go Bottle. A bottle that holds 4 go or 4*180ml. A 720ml bottle.

Yuki-bie - 雪冷え - Yuki-bie, a term for saké temperature, is "snow chilled" (5°C / 41°F).

Links and Contacts

Equipment List: Links and prices listed below are as of 10-01-2010. These links and prices may, and probably will, change. The only real question is when. I give them only for your convenience.

12" Steamer - Need 1: ($30)

Example: <http://www.cpapc.com/store/12-Aluminum-Steamer-with-Steam-Bowl-Lid-P1382C188.aspx>

3.5 Quart Food Grade Fermenter Bucket - Need 1: ($2.50)

Example: <http://www.cpapc.com/store/WHITE-C71.aspx>

6.5 Gallon Food Grade Fermenter Bucket - Need 1: ($14.50)

Example: <http://www.northernbrewer.com/brewing/brewing-equipment/fermenting-equipment/buckets>

Fine weave straining bag – Need 1: (~$5.00)

Example: <http://www.northernbrewer.com/brewing/catalogsearch/result/?q=+bag&x=0&y=0>

Small press – Food Grade Polypropylene - Strictly optional:($130)

Example: <http://thecheesemaker.com/TwoGallonPress.htm>

1 Gallon Glass Jug - Need 6: ($4 each, so 6 for $24)

Example: <http://www.northernbrewer.com/brewing/1-gallon-jug.html>

Fermentation locks to go on the glass jugs - Need 6: ($1.10 each, so $6.60)

Example: <http://www.northernbrewer.com/brewing/brewing-equipment/fermenting-equipment/fermentation-locs/bubbler-air-lock.html>

Stoppers for jug mouth, will need to check size at purchase time: ($1.50 each, so $9)

Example: <http://www.northernbrewer.com/brewing/brewing-equipment/fermenting-equipment/stoppers-bungs>

Auto Siphon (from Fermtech) / Racking Cane - Need 1: ($9)

Example: <http://www.northernbrewer.com/brewing/brewing-equipment/siphoning-equipment/racking-canes/auto-siphon-5-16.html>

3/8" ID Siphon Hose (to match racking cane OD) - Need 6-7 feet: ($0.35 per foot = $2.45)

Example: <http://www.northernbrewer.com/brewing/3-8-id-siphon-hose.html>

Hydrometer - Nice to have 1: ($6)

Example: <http://www.northernbrewer.com/brewing/brewing-equipment/testing-measuring/hydrometers-refractometers/triple-scale-hydrometer.html>

Hydrometer Jar - Nice to have 1: ($4)

Example: <http://www.northernbrewer.com/brewing/brewing-equipment/testing-measuring/hydrometers-refractometers/economy-test-jar.html>

Cleaning - Star San - I use BTF Iodophor but I think there is a problem shipping it. ($5 4oz. or $9 1/2Liter)

Example: <http://www.mainbrew.com/pages/sterilizers.html>

Links and Contacts

Cooler / Incubator for making koji: ($110)

Example:
<http://www.amazon.com/dp/B000Q73C66?s=appliances&ie=UTF8?tag=homebcom024-20>

Temperature Controller – Johnson Controller: ($79)

Example:
<http://morebeer.com/view_product/16670/102282/Johnson_Digital_Temperature_Controller_Wired>

Index

acidity. 20, 63, 79, 81, 119, 127, 146, 174, 176, 177, 179, 183, 187, 188, 204

air lock 14

Akita Komachi 43, 44

alcohol 1, 2, 7, 8, 9, 17, 19, 48, 59, 62, 63, 74, 75, 78, 107, 117, 120, 127, 135, 136, 145, 146, 151, 152, 153, 154, 155, 156, 161, 168, 169, 170, 171, 172, 191, 193, 195, 196, 197, 200, 202, 204, 205, 208, 209

Alpha-amylase 52

amelioration 37, 161, 162

amino acid . 52, 55, 56, 81, 152, 178, 179, 180, 181, 182, 185, 186

Amino acid 119, 165, 178, 193

amino sando 81, 178, 181

Amino sando 81

amylopectin 45, 54

amylose 42, 43, 45

aroma 1, 57, 58, 59, 81, 83, 105, 192, 196

Aspergillus Awamori 49, 200

Aspergillus Kawachi 49, 205

Aspergillus Oryzae 7, 49, 52, 107, 198, 199

auto siphon 15

Balling 73, 74

Baume 73, 74, 75, 76

Beni Koji 49

Beta-amylase 52

Bleach 86, 87

Blue Rose 42

Brix 73, 74, 171, 173

Calrose 43, 44

Calrose 76 .... 43, 44

Carolina Gold 40, 41, 42

Carolina White 40

Central Brewers Union 62, 63, 65

Chinriki 41, 42

Coloro 42, 43

Colusa 42

Daiginjo... 2, 5, 46, 93, 151, 158, 194

Daishichi 89, 92, 147

diacetyl 161, 192

enzymes 1, 7, 8, 9, 52, 53, 55, 56, 57, 95, 102, 105, 107, 111, 119, 131, 137, 145, 152, 169, 195, 199, 200, 201

Epsom salts 27, 28, 112, 120, 124, 128, 132, 139

fermentation..3, 5, 12, 50, 55, 59, 61, 62, 64, 74, 79, 101, 107, 111, 118,

127, 145, 148, 157, 169, 199, 201, 205, 212
fermentor 14, 31, 32, 34, 142, 143
first koji, second moto, third moromi 196
formalin 178, 179, 181, 186
Fuchu Homare Brewery 40
Futsu Shu 2
Gamma-amylase 52
Ginjo 2, 46, 48, 63, 92, 151, 194, 195, 208
Glucose 53
Gohyakumangoku 39
Hatsuzoe 8, 30, 31, 135, 139, 141, 195
Hiochi-kin 191, 192
Hitomebore 40, 43, 44, 93, 94, 95, 96
Honduras 41, 42
Honjozo 2, 46, 48, 93, 151, 152, 154, 155, 156, 196, 208
hydrometer . 17, 18, 19, 73, 165, 166, 168, 170, 171, 172, 173, 212
hydrometer jar 17
Ichi koji, ni moto, san tsukuri 196
Indica 39, 193
iodophor 21, 27, 87
iron 3, 5, 28, 30, 44, 68, 81, 101, 120, 124, 128
Japonica 39, 42, 44
Javanica 39
Junmai .. 2, 46, 48, 93, 151, 152, 197, 208
Junmai Daiginjo 93

kimoto 3, 79, 111, 116, 119, 120, 122, 123, 126, 134, 195, 197, 206, 208, 209
Kiushu 41, 42
koji 1, 2, 3, 5, 7, 8, 23, 25, 26, 27, 29, 30, 31, 32, 33, 48, 49, 50, 52, 55, 57, 58, 60, 61, 68, 81, 95, 101, 102, 104, 105, 106, 107, 108, 111, 113, 115, 118, 119, 120, 121, 123, 124, 125, 128, 129, 130, 131, 133, 135, 137, 138, 139, 140, 141, 142, 145, 151, 152, 169, 193, 194, 195, 196, 197, 198, 199, 201, 204, 205, 208, 209
koji-kin 7, 50, 51, 104, 106, 107, 108, 198, 205
Ko-on-Toka 131
Koshihikari 40, 43, 44
Kurabito 5, 200
Lactic acid 27, 79, 116, 206
magnesium 5, 27, 44, 46, 70, 71, 112, 115, 139
magnesium sulfate 70
Maltose 54
Milling 46, 89, 96, 97
Miyamizu 67, 68, 69, 70, 200
molarity 177, 182, 184, 187, 188
mole 53, 176, 182, 189
Moromi . 3, 8, 9, 29, 33, 64, 111, 115, 122, 126, 130, 133, 135, 142, 145, 146, 147, 149, 195, 197, 200, 201, 203, 207, 208
Morton Salt Substitute .. 27, 112, 115

moto ... 3, 7, 8, 12, 16, 25, 27, 28, 29, 30, 31, 60, 68, 70, 79, 80, 85, 101, 106, 111, 112, 113, 114, 115, 116, 117, 118, 119, 120, 121, 122, 123, 124, 125, 126, 127, 128, 129, 130, 131, 132, 133, 134, 135, 136, 137, 139, 145, 146, 191, 193, 196, 197, 198, 199, 200, 204, 206, 207, 208, 209

Moyashi 49, 50, 201

multiple parallel fermentation ... 169, 195

mycelia 51, 58, 105, 106

mycelium 50

Nakazoe 8, 31, 33, 135, 141, 142, 201

Nurihaze 106

Nurihaze koji 106

Omachi 39, 40

Oryza Sativa 39

pasteurization 16, 25, 36, 38, 161, 162, 192, 196

PBW 86, 87

Peptidases 52

Percarbonates 86

Phenolphthalein 174, 183

Plato 73, 74, 75, 76, 77, 78

Polishing 89, 90, 91

potassium chloride .. 27, 70, 112, 115, 139

Powder Brewery Wash 86

Protease 52

racking cane 15, 212

refractometer ... 17, 78, 171, 172, 173

refractometers 171, 212

Sakabukuro 12

Sakamai 40, 203

Sake Meter Value 17, 73, 165, 202

Salmon Lusk "Sol" Wright 42

sando 79, 81, 146, 174, 178, 179, 180, 181, 185, 193, 204

sanitizer ... 21, 27, 28, 31, 34, 87, 129

Sanzo Shu 2

Seaman A. Knapp 41

seigiku 50

Seimai 89, 204

shokumai 39, 205

SMV ... 17, 37, 73, 74, 75, 76, 77, 78, 79, 162, 165, 166, 168, 202

Sodium Hydroxide 174, 178, 187

Soe 135, 138

Sohaze 106

Sohaze koji 106

sokujo 3, 7, 79, 80, 85, 111, 112, 119, 120, 127, 130, 131, 134

special designation sake .. 2, 151, 208

specific gravity 17, 35, 37, 73, 74, 76, 78, 165, 166, 168, 169, 170, 171, 172, 173, 202

Star San 86, 87, 212

starter mash 3, 112

steamer 12, 29, 30, 31, 32, 33, 34, 103, 129, 132

Sterilization 86

stopper 14

Succinic 80, 176, 177, 180

Sulfatases 52

tane-koji 49
temperate Japonica 42
Titratable Acidity 176
titration 175, 178, 179, 181, 183, 185, 186, 188
Tomezoe 8, 33, 135, 142, 208
Tropical Japonica 39
Tsukihaze 106
Tsukihaze koji 106
TwinBird 93, 94, 95, 96
Wataribune 40, 41, 42
William W. Mackie 42
Yamadanishiki 40
yamahai 3, 79, 80, 85, 123, 126, 134, 206, 208

yeast .. 1, 2, 3, 7, 8, 25, 27, 28, 29, 30, 48, 49, 52, 54, 55, 57, 59, 60, 61, 62, 63, 64, 65, 66, 68, 79, 81, 85, 86, 107, 111, 112, 113, 115, 116, 117, 118, 119, 120, 122, 124, 125, 126, 127, 128, 129, 130, 131, 132, 133, 134, 136, 137, 139, 140, 145, 149, 152, 157, 161, 169, 193, 195, 197, 198, 199, 200, 201, 205, 206, 208
Yeast 59
Yeast nutrient 27
yellow koji 49, 198

Printed in Poland
by Amazon Fulfillment
Poland Sp. z o.o., Wrocław

21408800R00131